Gooseberry Patch
From our Kitchen to Yours

Our Best One-Bowl Meals

Comforting one-bowl meals perfect
for quick and healthy breakfasts,
lunches & dinners!

*To everyone who wants a
simple, comforting meal.*

Gooseberry Patch
An imprint of Globe Pequot
246 Goose Lane
Guilford, CT 06437

www.gooseberrypatch.com
1 800 854 6673

••••••••••••••••••••••

Do you have a tried & true recipe...
tip, craft or memory that you'd like to
see featured in a **Gooseberry Patch**
cookbook? Visit our website at
www.gooseberrypatch.com and
follow the easy steps to submit
your favorite family recipe.

Or send them to us at:
Gooseberry Patch
PO Box 812
Columbus, OH 43216-0812

Don't forget to include the number
of servings your recipe makes, plus
your name, address, phone number
and email address. If we select your
recipe, your name will appear right
along with it... and you'll receive a
FREE copy of the book!

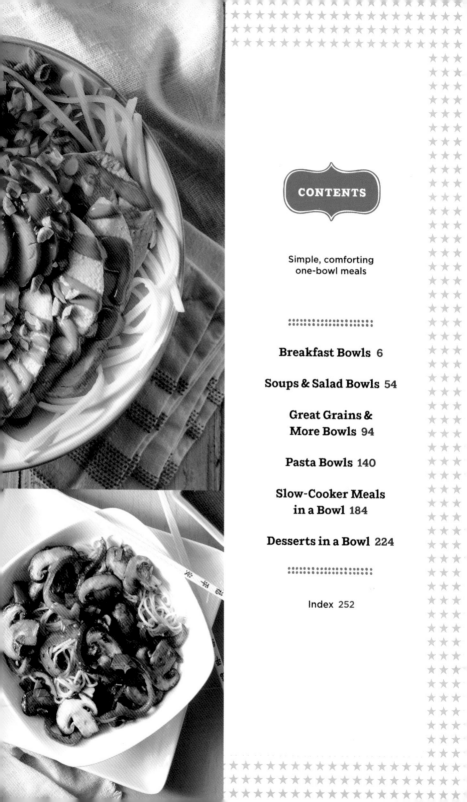

CONTENTS

Simple, comforting
one-bowl meals

::::::::::::::::::::::

::::::::::::::::::::::

Our Favorite One-Bowl Meals

Whether it's for breakfast, lunch or dinner, there's nothing more comforting than cooking up a big bowl of something hearty and delicious. Filled with grains, noodles, veggies or meat, one-bowl meals are perfect for a simple and satisfying meal.

There's no wrong way to whip up a one-bowl meal, so have some fun! Consider our recipes just a starting place to create meals your family will love, using their favorite ingredients. Here are a few tips for making one-bowl meals memorable and delicious:

Start with the base: Pasta, noodles, rice, quinoa, oats, greens, yogurt... the base of your bowl can be anything you like. This sets the stage for the whole meal.

Add your protein: Poached eggs, grilled shrimp, fried chicken, spicy black beans, chopped nuts...what are you in the mood for?

Add-ins: Color and texture are important in one-bowl meals. Shredded carrots, diced tomatoes and green onions are just a few of the colorful veggies you can add to a bowl. Purple cabbage, blueberries, strawberries, the choices and flavor combinations are endless!

Spice it up: A dash of salt & pepper may be all you need, but consider other flavor boosters such as hot pepper sauce, pickle relish or spicy brown mustard.

Add some crunch: From croutons and crunchy apples to toasted nuts or seeds, a little crunch adds great texture to any bowl.

Top it off: A dollop of sour cream, drizzle of dressing, splash of cream, sprinkle of chopped fresh herbs...little touches can add big flavor. These toppings are easy to customize too. Grated Parmesan cheese, crumbled feta, shredded Cheddar...pick your favorite!

The most important thing to remember when creating your one-bowl meals? Have fun!

Black Bean Breakfast Bowls, Page 16

CHAPTER ONE

Breakfast Bowls

Melon-Berry Bowls, Page 28

Rita's Turkey Hash, Page 52

Jennifer Gutermuth, Oshkosh, WI

Veggie, Egg & Rice Breakfast Bowls

I love eating veggies for breakfast! I use whatever is in my kitchen...red pepper, zucchini, green beans. They are all good in this bowl.

Makes 4 servings

1 T. olive oil
1 lb. asparagus, cut into bite-sized pieces
3 c. fresh spinach leaves
Honey Mustard Dressing
3 c. cabbage, shredded
1-1/2 c. cooked brown rice, warmed
1/2 c. hummus
1 avocado, peeled, pitted and diced
4 eggs
Garnish: chopped pecans, pumpkin seeds

Heat oil in a skillet over medium-high heat. Add asparagus and sauté for 4 to 5 minutes, stirring occasionally, until tender; set side. In a separate bowl, combine spinach and Honey-Mustard dressing. Add asparagus, cabbage and rice; toss until combined. Divide spinach mixture evenly among 4 bowls. Top each with hummus and avocado; set aside. To poach eggs, fill a skillet with water and bring to a simmer over medium-high heat. Swirl water with a spoon and gently slide in each egg from a saucer. Cook until set, about 2 minutes. Use a slotted spoon to remove each egg to a bowl. Garnish as desired.

Honey-Mustard Dressing:

2 T. olive oil
2 T. lemon juice
2 t. mustard
2 T. honey
1 clove garlic, minced
salt and pepper to taste

In a small bowl, whisk together all ingredients.

★ HOT TIP ★ If you prefer cooked cabbage over raw, toss the cabbage in along with the asparagus. It'll cook up in no time!

Veggie, Egg & Rice Breakfast Bowls

JoAnn, Gooseberry Patch

Cinnamon-Apple Quinoa Breakfast Bowls

This makes a hearty breakfast, but sometimes we have this for a light dinner too.

Makes 4 servings

1/2 c. quinoa, uncooked, rinsed
   and drained
1-1/4 c. almond milk
1/2 t. vanilla extract
1/4 t. cinnamon
1/8 t. nutmeg
1/8 t. salt
Optional: almond milk, maple syrup,
   chopped pecans, shredded coconut

Prepare Maple Roasted Apples. Meanwhile, in a saucepan over medium heat, stir together quinoa, almond milk, vanilla, spices and salt. Bring to a boil; reduce heat to low. Simmer for 10 to 15 minutes, until quinoa is cooked through and liquid has been absorbed. Remove from heat; cover and let stand for 5 to 10 minutes. Fluff with a fork. To serve, divide warm quinoa among 4 bowls; top with apple mixture. Garnish as desired.

Maple Roasted Apples:

1 T. coconut oil, melted
2 T. maple syrup
1/2 t. vanilla extract
1/4 t. cinnamon
1/8 t. nutmeg
2 Gala apples, quartered and cored

In a bowl, whisk together coconut oil and maple syrup; stir in vanilla and spices. Add apples; toss until coated. Arrange apples on a parchment paper-lined rimmed baking sheet. Bake at 375 degrees for 20 to 25 minutes, basting with pan juices once or twice, until golden. Cool slightly.

★ SIMPLE INGREDIENT SWAP ★
Out of quinoa? Try using brown rice instead. It's just as tasty and filling, too.

Cinnamon-Apple Quinoa Breakfast Bowls

Bob Gurlinger, Kearney, NE

Strawberry-Banana Smoothie Breakfast Bowls

These are so easy to customize. We try different fruit combinations all the time. Strawberry-banana is still my favorite.

Makes 2 servings

2 c. frozen strawberries
2 bananas, sliced and frozen
1 c. almond milk
2 T. creamy peanut butter
1 c. fresh spinach leaves
Garnish: shredded coconut, pecans, blueberries, strawberries, granola, maple syrup

In a blender, combine all ingredients except garnish; process well until smooth. Divide between 2 bowls; garnish as desired.

Lita Hardy, Santa Cruz, CA

Best Brunch Casserole

My family & friends have been enjoying this dish for over 30 years!

Makes 8 servings

4 c. croutons
2 c. shredded Cheddar cheese
8 eggs, beaten
4 c. milk
1 t. salt
1 t. pepper
2 t. mustard
1 T. dried, minced onion
6 slices bacon, crisply cooked and crumbled

Spread croutons in the bottom of a greased 13"x9" baking pan; sprinkle with cheese. Set aside. Whisk eggs, milk, salt, pepper, mustard and onion together; pour over cheese. Sprinkle bacon on top; bake at 325 degrees until set, about 55 to 60 minutes.

Strawberry-Banana Smoothie Breakfast Bowls

Linda Picard, Newport, OR

Savory Oatmeal Bowls with Egg, Bacon & Kale

This is so warm and comforting first thing in the morning. If you like it spicy, the hot pepper sauce on the veggies makes it even better.

Makes 2 servings

2 slices bacon, diced
1 bunch kale, thinly sliced
1/2 c. tomato, diced
1 t. red wine vinegar
1/8 t. salt
1 c. cooked steel-cut oats
1/3 c. avocado, peeled, pitted
 and diced
1 t. olive oil
2 eggs
1/8 t. pepper
Optional: 1/2 t. hot pepper sauce

In a large skillet over medium heat, cook bacon until almost crisp, stirring occasionally. Add kale; cook for 2 to 4 minutes, until wilted. Stir in tomato, vinegar and salt. Divide oats evenly between 2 bowls. Top with kale mixture and avocado; set aside. Wipe skillet clean with a paper towel; return to medium heat. Add oil and swirl to coat. Crack eggs into skillet, one at a time; cook for 2 minutes. Cover and cook for one minute, or until whites are set. Top each bowl with one egg. Sprinkle with pepper and hot sauce, if using.

★ SIMPLE INGREDIENT SWAP ★ Have leftover spinach from last night's salad? Swap out the kale for spinach in these bowls. Delicious!

Savory Oatmeal Bowls with Egg, Bacon & Kale

Vickie, Gooseberry Patch

Black Bean Breakfast Bowls

I love black beans, so finding a tasty way to have them for breakfast makes me happy. Sometimes I sprinkle a bit of chopped, fresh cilantro on top for extra flavor.

Makes 2 servings

2 T. olive oil
4 eggs, beaten
15-1/2 oz. can black beans, drained and rinsed
1 avocado, peeled, pitted and sliced
1/4 c. shredded Cheddar cheese
1/4 c. favorite salsa
salt and pepper to taste

Heat oil in a skillet over medium heat. Add eggs and scramble as desired, 3 to 5 minutes; remove from heat. Place beans in a microwave-safe bowl. Microwave on high until warm, one to 2 minutes. To serve, divide beans among 2 bowls; top each bowl with eggs, avocado, cheese and salsa. Season with salt and pepper.

Jill Valentine, Jackson, TN

Sausage Brunch Bake

An oh-so-easy brunch dish that's really tasty.

Serves 8 to 10

3 c. herb-flavored croutons
8-oz. pkg. shredded Cheddar cheese, divided
1/2 lb. ground pork sausage, browned and drained
4 eggs, beaten
2-1/2 c. milk, divided
3/4 t. dry mustard
10-3/4 oz. can cream of mushroom soup
32-oz. pkg. frozen shredded hashbrowns, thawed

Spread croutons in an aluminum foil-lined 13"x9" baking pan. Top croutons with 1-1/2 cups cheese and sausage; set aside. Combine eggs, 2 cups milk and mustard; pour over all. Cover and refrigerate overnight. Combine soup with remaining milk; pour over mixture. Spread hashbrowns over top; sprinkle with remaining cheese. Bake, uncovered, at 325 degrees for one hour.

Black Bean Breakfast Bowls

Jennifer Howard, Santa Fe, NM

Breezy Brunch Skillet

Try this all-in-one breakfast on your next camp-out! Just set the skillet on a grate over hot coals.

Serves 4 to 6

6 slices bacon, diced
6 c. frozen diced potatoes
3/4 c. green pepper, chopped
1/2 c. onion, chopped
1 t. salt
1/4 t. pepper
4 to 6 eggs
1/2 c. shredded Cheddar cheese

In a large cast-iron skillet over medium-high heat, cook bacon until crisp. Drain and set aside, reserving 2 tablespoon drippings in skillet. Add potatoes, green pepper, onion, salt and pepper to drippings. Cook and stir for 2 minutes. Cover and cook for about 15 minutes, stirring occasionally, until potatoes are golden and tender. With a spoon, make 4 to 6 wells in potato mixture. Crack one egg into each well, taking care not to break the yolks. Cover and cook over low heat for 8 to 10 minutes, until eggs are completely set. Sprinkle with cheese and crumbled bacon.

★ TIME-SAVING SHORTCUT ★ In a hurry? Save a little time by using frozen diced potatoes with onions and peppers already added!

Breezy Brunch Skillet

David Wink, Gooseberry Patch

Oatmeal Cookie Breakfast Bowl

This is great for breakfast, but good enough for dessert too!

Makes 1 serving

1 egg, beaten
1-1/4 c. milk
2/3 c. quick-cooking oats, uncooked
2 T. raisins
1 T. brown sugar, packed
1 t. vanilla extract
1 t. butter
1/4 t. cinnamon
salt to taste
Optional: additional milk, chopped pecans, raisins

Whisk together egg and milk in a microwave-safe bowl; add remaining ingredients and mix well. Microwave on high for one minute; stir and microwave for one minute more. Stir; microwave until cooked, about one minute. Serve topped with milk and pecans, if desired.

Gloria Bills, Plymouth, MI

Overnight Blueberry French Toast

This delicious recipe has become a holiday tradition at our house...my husband and children love it! It's easy to make the night before, then in the morning, just pop it in the oven.

Serves 6 to 8

1 baguette loaf, sliced 1-inch thick
6 eggs
3 c. milk
1 c. brown sugar, packed and divided
vanilla extract to taste
nutmeg to taste
1/4 c. chopped pecans
2 c. blueberries
Optional: maple syrup

Arrange baguette slices in a lightly greased 13"x9" baking pan; set aside. In a large bowl, whisk together eggs, milk, 3/4 cup brown sugar, vanilla and nutmeg. Pour mixture evenly over baguette slices. Cover and chill overnight. Just before baking, sprinkle remaining brown sugar, pecans and blueberries over top. Bake, uncovered, at 350 degrees for 30 minutes, until golden and bubbly. Serve with maple syrup, if desired.

Oatmeal Cookie Breakfast Bowl

Fern Bruner, Palo Alto, CA

Butterscotch Granola

The best granola you'll ever taste! Sprinkle it over berry yogurt for a wonderful breakfast treat.

Makes 5 quarts

10 c. long-cooking oats, uncooked
2 sleeves graham crackers, crushed
2 c. sweetened flaked coconut
1 c. pecans, finely chopped
3/4 c. brown sugar, packed
1 t. baking soda
1 t. salt

2 c. butter, melted
16-oz. pkg. butterscotch chips

Mix together all ingredients except butterscotch chips in a greased deep 13"x9" baking pan. Bake, uncovered, at 300 degrees for 40 minutes, stirring every 10 minutes. Add butterscotch chips during the last 5 minutes; mix well after melted to distribute evenly. Cool; store in an airtight container.

★ SKINNY SECRET ★ Serving brunch? Try a breakfast trifle! Layer creamy yogurt, crunchy granola and juicy fresh berries in a clear glass bowl...perfect for brunch guests with lighter appetites.

Butterscotch Granola

Jennifer McClure, Lebanon, IN

Southern Veggie Brunch Casserole

Our family always has this breakfast dish for dinner, and it's fondly called "brinner" by our two children.

Serves 6 to 8

1 lb. ground pork sausage, browned and drained
1/2 c. green onions, chopped
1 green pepper, diced
1 red pepper, diced
1 jalapeño pepper, seeded and diced
2 tomatoes, chopped
2 c. shredded mozzarella cheese
1 c. biscuit baking mix

1 doz. eggs, beaten
1 c. milk
1/2 t. dried oregano
1/2 t. salt
1/4 t. pepper

In a greased 3-quart casserole dish, layer sausage, onions, peppers, tomatoes and cheese. In a large bowl, whisk together remaining ingredients; pour over cheese. Bake, uncovered, at 350 degrees for 55 to 60 minutes, until set and top is golden. Let stand for 10 minutes before serving.

★ SIMPLE INGREDIENT SWAP ★ If hot peppers are too spicy for your crowd, try using a few tablespoons of mild, diced green chiles instead. You'll get plenty of flavor, and a lot less heat.

Southern Veggie Brunch Casserole

Beth Bennett, Stratham, NH

Fruited Orange Yogurt

A smooth and crunchy, sweet and zingy breakfast you can enjoy on the go.

Serves 4 to 6

8-oz. container mascarpone
  cheese
32-oz. container plain yogurt
1/3 c. sugar
juice and zest of 2 oranges
Garnish: granola, blueberries,
  raspberries, sliced bananas

In a bowl, combine cheese, yogurt and sugar. Stir in juice and zest. Sprinkle granola over top. Serve with fresh fruit.

Vickie, Gooseberry Patch

Angel Hair Brunch Frittata

Whenever my friends come for brunch, this dish is a must! Very easy to make and you can vary it with veggies and cheeses you have on hand.

Makes 6 servings

8-oz. pkg. angel hair pasta, uncooked
3 eggs, lightly beaten
1/4 c. milk
1/2 c. grated Parmesan cheese
1/2 t. salt
1/8 t. pepper
3/4 c. provolone cheese, shredded
1/2 c. asparagus, chopped
1/2 c. tomato, chopped
1/2 c. sliced black olives, drained
Garnish: tomato and garlic pasta
  sauce, warmed

Cook pasta according to package directions; drain. Meanwhile, in a bowl, whisk together eggs, milk, Parmesan cheese, salt and pepper; mix well. Add cooked pasta to egg mixture; mix gently and spread in a lightly greased 9" pie plate. Top with provolone cheese and vegetables. Cover with aluminum foil. Bake at 350 degrees for 20 minutes. Uncover; bake 15 minutes longer. Cut into wedges and serve warm, topped with pasta sauce.

Fruited Orange Yogurt

Jill Ball, Highland, UT

Melon-Berry Bowls

I am always looking for quick, healthy and yummy breakfast ideas for my teenagers. This one has become a favorite!

Serves 2 to 4

1 honeydew melon, halved and
   seeded
6-oz. container favorite-flavor
   yogurt
1/2 c. blueberries
1 c. granola cereal

Use a melon baller to scoop honeydew into balls. Combine melon balls with remaining ingredients. Spoon into individual bowls to serve.

Sandra Leasure, Circleville, OH

Sandi's Special Apple Oatmeal

An easy-to-make breakfast treat! If you like thicker oatmeal, add a little more oats; for thinner, add more milk.

Makes 6 servings

5 c. milk
3 c. whole-grain quick-cooking
   oats, uncooked
1-1/2 c. apples, peeled, cored
   and diced
1/2 c. light brown sugar, packed
1 t. cinnamon
Optional: milk, brown sugar

In a heavy saucepan over medium heat, bring milk to a boil. Stir in oats, apples, brown sugar and cinnamon. Cook for one minute, stirring occasionally. Remove from heat; cover and let stand for 2 to 3 minutes. Serve topped with milk and additional brown sugar, if desired.

Melon-Berry Bowls

Elizabeth McCord, Bartlett, TN

Perfect Purple Smoothie

Smoothies are one of my favorite treats and I love creating new variations. This one is a favorite!

Makes 2 servings

1-1/2 c. frozen mixed fruit
1-1/4 c. frozen blueberries
1 to 1-1/2 c. orange juice
1/2 c. milk
1/4 c. rolled oats, uncooked
1/2 c. vanilla Greek yogurt or regular yogurt
6 ice cubes

Combine all ingredients into a blender. Blend very well until oats are thoroughly mixed in. Serve in tall glasses or bowls.

★ TIME-SAVING SHORTCUT ★
Are breakfast smoothies a favorite at your house? Mix them up the night before, then pour into canning jars and tuck in the fridge. Perfect portions, ready to go!

Janis Parr, Ontario, Canada

Country Brunch Medley

This is the perfect make-ahead breakfast casserole!

Serves 10 to 12

4 c. bread, cubed
8-oz. pkg. shredded Cheddar cheese
8 to 10 slices bacon, crisply cooked and coarsely chopped
1/2 c. mushrooms, chopped
1 c. tomatoes, chopped
1/3 c. white onion, chopped
1 c. cooked ham, cubed
10 eggs, well beaten
4 c. milk
1 t. dry mustard
1/4 t. onion powder
1 t. salt
1/4 t. pepper

The day before serving, spread bread cubes in the bottom of a greased deep 13"x9" baking pan. Sprinkle cheese over top. Layer with bacon, vegetables and ham; set aside. In a large bowl, beat together remaining ingredients. Carefully pour milk mixture over layered mixture in pan; do not stir. Cover and refrigerate for 24 hours. Bake, uncovered, at 325 degrees for 50 to 60 minutes, until set in the center. Serve piping hot.

Perfect Purple Smoothie

Julie Dossantos, Fort Pierce, FL

Autumn Morning Smoothie

Our family loves to make breakfast smoothies. After baking pie pumpkins, I decided to try making smoothies for Thanksgiving morning. They were a hit! Now we enjoy them all autumn.

Makes 2 servings

1/2 c. fresh pumpkin purée or
   canned pumpkin
3/4 c. papaya, peeled, seeded
   and cubed

2 bananas, sliced
1/2 c. low-fat vanilla yogurt
1/4 c. orange juice
4 ice cubes
1-1/2 t. cinnamon
Garnish: additional cinnamon

Add all ingredients except garnish to a blender. Process until smooth; pour into 2 tall glasses or bowls. Top each with a sprinkle of cinnamon.

★ KID-FRIENDLY ★ Fruit-filled smoothies are delicious and good for you! They're perfect for kids who don't have much appetite when they get up in the morning.

Autumn Morning Smoothie

Lisa Ann Panzino DiNunzio,
Vineland, NJ

Peach Pie Smoothie

Refreshing and oh-so good!

Makes 2 servings

1/4 c. almond milk or regular
   milk
1 c. non-fat plain Greek yogurt
1 c. frozen unsweetened peaches
1 to 2 T. honey or pure maple
   syrup
1/2 t. vanilla extract
1/4 t. cinnamon
1/8 t. nutmeg
1 c. ice cubes
Garnish: nutmeg, sliced peaches

Combine all ingredients into a
blender and blend until smooth.
Serve in tall glasses or bowls.
Garnish as desired.

Hannah Hilgendorf, Nashotah, WI

Peachy Baked Oatmeal

I found this recipe and tweaked it
until it was just right for us. It was
an instant hit! It's also yummy made
with cranberry chutney or other
mostly-firm fruit instead of peaches.

Makes 6 servings

2 eggs, beaten
1/2 c. brown sugar, packed
1-1/2 t. baking powder
1/4 t. salt
1-1/2 t. cinnamon
1/2 t. nutmeg
1-1/2 t. vanilla extract
3/4 c. milk
3 c. long-cooking oats,
   uncooked
1/3 c. oil
16-oz. can sliced peaches,
   partially drained
Garnish: warm milk

In a bowl, combine eggs, brown sugar,
baking powder, salt, spices and vanilla;
beat well. Add remaining ingredients
except garnish; mix thoroughly. Spoon
into a greased 8"x8" baking pan. Bake at
375 degrees for 20 to 25 minutes, until
center is set. Serve in bowls, topped
with warm milk.

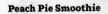
Peach Pie Smoothie

Courtney Stultz, Weir, KS

Banana Pudding Smoothie

Smoothies are great for quick nutrition, especially for busy families! This one is wonderful because it tastes like a milkshake... only healthier! Our whole family loves it.

Makes 1 serving

1 banana, cut into chunks
8-oz. container plain or vanilla yogurt
3/4 c. coconut milk or almond milk
1/4 c. chopped almonds
1/2 t. cinnamon
1/8 t. vanilla extract
1/2 c. ice, if desired

Combine all ingredients in a blender. Process for about 30 to 45 seconds, until completely smooth. Makes one serving.

Phyllis Peters, Three Rivers, MI

Mom's Red Flannel Hash

If you love beets, you'll love this hash!

Serves 4 to 6

12-oz. can corned beef, coarsely chopped
2 c. beets, peeled, cooked and chopped
2 c. potatoes, peeled, cooked and chopped
1/2 c. butter, melted

Toss all ingredients together. Pour into a greased 2-quart casserole dish. Bake, uncovered, at 350 degrees for 40 minutes.

★ FREEZE IT ★ Save bananas that are getting too ripe. Peel, cut into chunks, wrap in plastic wrap and tuck in the freezer. Later they can be tossed into smoothies...no thawing needed.

Banana Pudding Smoothie

Shirl Parsons, Cape Carteret, NC

Banana-Mango Soy Smoothie

A cool refreshing pick-me-up drink... especially good for those who can't tolerate milk!

Makes 6 servings

2 c. vanilla or plain soy milk
2 to 3 bananas, sliced and
　frozen
6 mangoes, pitted, peeled,
　cubed and frozen
1 T. honey, or to taste

Combine all ingredients in a blender. Blend on high setting until smooth and frothy. Pour into tall glasses or bowls.

Patty Laughery, Moses Lake, WA

Early-Riser Breakfast

This has become a tradition at Easter and Christmas because it's so easy to prepare the night before and everyone loves it!

Makes 8 servings

8 slices bread, cubed
1 c. shredded Cheddar cheese
1 c. shredded Monterey Jack cheese
1-1/2 lbs. ground pork sausage,
　browned and drained
4 eggs, beaten
3 c. milk, divided
10-3/4 oz. can cream of
　mushroom soup
3/4 t. dry mustard

Arrange bread in an ungreased 13"x9" baking pan; sprinkle with cheeses and sausage. Set aside. Mix eggs and 2-1/2 cups milk together; pour over bread. Cover with aluminum foil; refrigerate overnight. Combine remaining ingredients; pour over bread mixture. Bake, uncovered, at 300 degrees for 1-1/2 hours.

Banana-Mango Soy Smoothie

Kelly Gray, Weston, WV

Christmas Eggs

I used the eggs-in-a-hole idea for this recipe. My boys know it's Christmas when I start serving these eggs! They're so pretty on a plate at Christmastime, but fun to eat year 'round too. If you're not a fan of grits, you could serve them over buttered toast.

Makes 6 servings

1 red pepper, sliced into 6, 1/4-inch thick rings
6 eggs
salt and pepper to taste
cooked grits
Garnish: chopped fresh parsley

Spray a large sauté pan or skillet generously with non-stick vegetable spray. Add red pepper rings and cook over medium-high heat, about 5 minutes on each side. Crack an egg into each pepper ring. Reduce heat to low. Cook to desired doneness, about 5 to 6 minutes. Season with salt and pepper. Use a spatula to remove eggs from pan; arrange over cooked grits and sprinkle with parsley.

★ TIME-SAVING SHORTCUT ★ Cook up a crock of overnight grits...creamy and perfect every time! Following the package directions, add the desired amount of grits to a slow cooker (long-cooking grits work best) and twice the amount of water as specified. Sprinkle with salt. Cover and cook on low setting for 7 to 8 hours, stirring in more water toward the end of cooking time, if needed. Top with butter, shredded cheese or a splash of cream.

Christmas Eggs

Amy Bradsher, Roxboro, NC

Peanut Butter & Chocolate Baked Oatmeal

This baked oatmeal tastes almost like a giant oatmeal cookie! It's soft and moist, peanutty and swirled throughout with melted chocolate. We love to eat it with a fork and a big glass of milk. It keeps my family's tummies full until lunchtime.

Serves 5 to 6

3 c. quick-cooking oats,
  uncooked
1/4 c. brown sugar, packed
2 t. baking powder
3/4 t. salt
1 c. milk
2 eggs, beaten
2 T. butter, melted
2 t. vanilla extract
1/2 c. creamy peanut butter
1/2 c. semi-sweet chocolate
  chips

In a large bowl, stir together oats, brown sugar, baking powder and salt. Add milk, eggs, butter, vanilla and peanut butter; mix well. Fold in chocolate chips. Spread evenly in a greased 13"x9" baking pan. Bake, uncovered, at 350 degrees for 25 minutes. Serve warm.

★ SIMPLE INGREDIENT SWAP ★ **Quick-cooking oats are pre-cooked, dried, rolled and pressed slightly thinner than rolled oats. They cook more quickly than steel-cut or rolled oats, but retain less of their texture. Rolled oats can be used in place of quick-cooking oats, although it will require a little more cooking time.**

Peanut Butter & Chocolate Baked Oatmeal

Lisa Sett, Thousand Oaks, CA

Scrambled Egg in a Cup

This is my favorite "breakfast on the go" before I go to the gym. Comes out perfect every time! Easy for older kids to make for themselves...try it on an English muffin.

Makes 1 serving

1 egg
salt and pepper to taste
2 T. fresh spinach, chopped
Garnish: 1 to 2 t. shredded
   cheese, salsa, sliced green
   onion

Beat egg, salt and pepper well in a greased microwave-safe mug; add spinach. Microwave on high for one minute. Garnish as desired and serve from mug.

Kathy Unruh, Fresno, CA

Baked Garden Omelet

Here's one omelet you don't have to flip!

Serves 6 to 8

8 eggs, beaten
1 c. ricotta cheese
1/2 c. milk
1/2 t. dried basil
1/4 t. salt
1/4 t. fennel seed, crushed
1/4 t. pepper
10-oz. pkg. frozen spinach, thawed
   and drained
1 c. tomatoes, chopped
1 c. shredded mozzarella cheese
1/2 c. green onion, sliced
1/2 c. salami, diced

Whisk eggs and ricotta cheese together in a large mixing bowl; add milk, basil, salt, fennel seed and pepper. Fold in remaining ingredients; spread in a greased 13"x9" baking pan. Bake at 325 degrees until a knife inserted in the center removes clean, about 30 to 35 minutes; let stand 10 minutes before serving.

Scrambled Egg in a Cup

Karol Cannon, Sharpsville, IN

Pumpkin Pie Baked Oatmeal

This oatmeal brings back special memories of eating oatmeal as a child! Good warm out of the oven... it's even good cold. Enjoy!

Makes 9 servings

15-oz. can pumpkin
1/3 c. brown sugar, packed
1/3 c. egg whites, beaten
1-1/2 t. pumpkin pie spice
3/4 t. baking powder
1/4 t. salt
1-1/2 c. milk

2 c. steel-cut oats, uncooked
Optional: whipped topping or
  vanilla ice cream

In a bowl, whisk together pumpkin, brown sugar, egg whites, spice, baking powder and salt. Add milk; stir until well mixed. Stir in oats; spread in a greased 9"x9" baking pan. Cover with aluminum foil. Bake at 350 degrees for 30 minutes. Uncover; bake an additional 15 minutes. Serve warm, garnished as desired.

★ SIMPLE INGREDIENT SWAP ★ Prefer butternut squash over pumpkin? Simply swap out 2 cups cooked, pureed butternut squash for the pumpkin in this recipe. Easy and tasty!

Pumpkin Pie Baked Oatmeal

Jenny Poole, Salisbury, NC

Turkey-Spinach Quiche

This recipe is a holiday tradition at our house. I bake it in mini pie tins for a nice presentation...my guests love it.

Serves 4 to 6

1 lb. ground turkey sausage, browned and drained
3 c. shredded Cheddar cheese
10-oz. pkg. frozen chopped spinach, cooked and drained
6-1/2 oz. jar sliced mushrooms, drained
2/3 c. onion, chopped
1 c. mayonnaise
1 c. milk
4 eggs, beaten
1-1/4 c. biscuit baking mix
2 T. cornstarch

In a large bowl, mix together all ingredients. Pour into greased mini pie tins. Bake, uncovered, at 350 degrees for 20 minutes, or until golden and set.

Kathleen Kennedy, Renton, WA

Denver Scramble

All my menfolk love this dish! The recipe can easily be divided or multiplied depending on how many hungry diners you have. Add fresh fruit and buttered toast for a well-rounded meal.

Serves 4 to 6

3 to 4 T. butter
1 lb. thick-sliced cooked deli ham, diced
1 c. green or red peppers, diced
1 c. yellow onion, diced
6 eggs
1/4 c. milk
pepper to taste
1/2 c. shredded Cheddar cheese
Optional: diced tomatoes

Melt butter in a large skillet over medium heat until it starts to sizzle. Add ham, peppers and onion to skillet; cook until vegetables are crisp-tender. Meanwhile, whisk together eggs and milk in a bowl. Stir egg mixture into mixture in skillet; season with pepper. Reduce heat to medium-low. Cook until eggs are set, stirring occasionally, 4 to 5 minutes. Remove skillet from heat. Top with cheese; let stand for a minute, until cheese melts. Sprinkle with tomatoes, if desired.

Turkey-Spinach Quiche

Lisa Ann Panzino DiNunzio,
Vineland, NJ

Pumpkin Pie Smoothie

This smoothie can be put into a covered mug for breakfast on the go, or serve in a tall glass topped with whipped cream for the perfect drinkable dessert!

Makes 2 servings

3/4 c. milk or unsweetened
  almond milk
1/2 c. plain Greek yogurt
2 to 3 T. maple syrup or honey
1/2 c. canned pumpkin
1/2 t. vanilla extract
1/2 t. cinnamon
Optional: 1/8 t. nutmeg
1 c. ice cubes

Combine all ingredients in a blender; process until smooth.

Jennie Gist, Gooseberry Patch

Easy Egg Bake

I've made this dish often to share with friends. It just takes a few minutes to put together and pop in the oven! Change up the ingredients as you like... sometimes I'll omit the bacon.

Makes 8 servings

20-oz. pkg. refrigerated diced
  potatoes with onions
6-oz. pkg. precooked bacon
6 to 8 eggs, beaten
1/4 c. milk
salt and pepper to taste
8-oz. pkg. shredded sharp Cheddar
  cheese

Spray a 13"x9" baking pan with non-stick vegetable spray. Spread potatoes in pan. Using kitchen scissors, snip bacon into pieces over potatoes. Bake, uncovered, at 350 degrees for about 15 minutes; remove from oven. Whisk together eggs and milk; pour over baked layer. Sprinkle with salt, pepper and cheese. Return to oven, uncovered, for 25 to 30 minutes, until eggs are set and cheese is melted. Cut into squares.

★ SIMPLE INGREDIENT SWAP ★ **Out of honey? Agave nectar is a good substitute. It's sweeter than sugar and made from the agave plant. It's normally found in stores near the honey.**

Pumpkin Pie Smoothie

Rita Morgan, Pueblo, CO

Rita's Turkey Hash

This is my favorite hearty breakfast to serve every Black Friday, before my sisters and I head to the mall to do some serious shopping. Add a side of leftover cranberry sauce...delish!

Makes 4 servings

1 T. butter
1 T. vegetable oil
1 onion, chopped
1 red pepper, chopped
2 c. potatoes, peeled, cooked
   and diced
2 c. roast turkey, diced
1 t. fresh thyme
salt and pepper to taste

Melt butter with oil in a large, heavy skillet over medium heat. Add onion and red pepper. Sauté until onion is tender, about 5 minutes. Add remaining ingredients. Spread out mixture in skillet, pressing lightly to form an even layer. Cook 5 to 10 minutes, or until golden. Remove from heat. Spoon hash onto 4 plates. Top with Poached Eggs and serve immediately.

Poached Eggs:

1 T. white vinegar
4 eggs
salt and pepper to taste

Add several inches of water to a deep skillet or saucepan. Bring water to a simmer over medium-high heat. Stir in vinegar. Crack eggs, one at a time, into water. Cook just until whites are firm and yolks are still soft, about 3 to 4 minutes. Remove eggs with a slotted spoon. Sprinkle with salt and pepper.

★ HOT TIP ★ Poached eggs for a crowd! For each egg, add one tablespoon water to a muffin cup. Break an egg directly into each cup. Bake at 350 degrees, 11 to 13 minutes for runny yolks, a bit longer for firmer yolks. Remove from oven and let stand for one minute, then gently remove eggs with a slotted spoon.

Rita's Turkey Hash

Jambo, Page 68

CHAPTER TWO

Soups & Salad Bowls

Chicken Minestrone, Page 62

Italian Salad Bowl, Page 86

Amy Butcher, Columbus, GA

Ham & Potato Chowder

Crusty bread from the bakery makes this a comforting meal!

Makes 6 servings

1/4 c. butter
1 onion, chopped
3 cloves garlic, minced
1/4 c. green pepper, chopped
1/4 c. red pepper, chopped
2 carrots, peeled and diced
4 14-1/2 oz. cans chicken broth
4 c. redskin potatoes, quartered
1/4 t. nutmeg
1-1/2 t. dried thyme
2 T. all-purpose flour
2/3 c. water
2 c. milk
11-oz. can corn, drained
2 c. cooked ham, diced
oyster crackers

Melt butter in a large pot over medium heat; sauté onion, garlic, peppers and carrots until tender. Add broth, potatoes, nutmeg and thyme. Reduce heat; cover and simmer for 1-1/2 hours. Bring to a boil. Whisk flour and water together and slowly add to chowder. Boil until thickened. Remove from heat and slowly pour in milk; stir in corn and ham. Serve with oyster crackers.

Laura Witham, Anchorage, AK

Spicy Shrimp Noodle Bowl

Whenever my husband and I go out for Asian food, my favorite dishes are the noodle bowls. Here is my own version of a satisfying, spicy shrimp noodle bowl that you can make at home.

Serves 4 to 6

3 T. olive oil
1 leek, chopped
4 cloves garlic, minced
2 t. red pepper flakes
salt and pepper to taste
4 c. chicken broth
2 8-oz. bottles clam juice
8-oz. pkg. angel hair pasta, uncooked
1 lb. uncooked medium shrimp,
   peeled and cleaned

Heat a large deep skillet over medium heat; add oil. Add leek and seasonings; sauté for 3 minutes. Pour in broth and juice; bring to a boil. Turn down to a simmer. Add pasta to skillet and cook for 3 to 5 minutes, until tender. Add shrimp and cook 5 minutes more.

Ham & Potato Chowder

Becky Butler, Keller, TX

Apple-Walnut Chicken Salad

This tasty recipe uses the convenience of a roast chicken from your grocery store's deli...what a great time-saver!

Makes 6 servings

6 c. mixed field greens or baby greens
2 c. deli roast chicken, shredded
1/3 c. crumbled blue cheese
1/4 c. chopped walnuts, toasted
1 Fuji or Gala apple, cored and
   chopped

In a large salad bowl, toss together all ingredients. Drizzle Balsamic Apple Vinaigrette over salad, tossing gently to coat. Serve immediately.

Balsamic Apple Vinaigrette:

2 T. frozen apple juice concentrate
1 T. cider vinegar
1 T. white balsamic vinegar
1 t. Dijon mustard
1/4 t. garlic powder
1/3 c. olive oil

Whisk together all ingredients in a small bowl.

★ LOW-CAL ADD-ON ★ Add a healthy crunch to salads with a sprinkle of sunflower kernels or toasted pumpkin seeds.

Apple-Walnut Chicken Salad

Sandy Westendorp, Grand Rapids, MI

Pumpkin Chowder

This blend of everyday ingredients is anything but ordinary.

Makes 6 servings

1/2 lb. bacon, diced
2 c. onion, chopped
2 t. curry powder
2 T. all-purpose flour
1-lb. pie pumpkin, peeled, seeded
   and chopped
2 potatoes, peeled and cubed
4 c. chicken broth
1 c. half-and-half
salt and pepper to taste
Garnish: toasted pumpkin seeds,
   sliced green onions

Brown bacon in a stockpot over medium heat for 5 minutes; add onion. Sauté for 10 minutes; add curry powder and flour, stirring until smooth and creamy, about 5 minutes. Add pumpkin, potatoes and broth; simmer until pumpkin and potatoes are tender, about 15 minutes. Pour in half-and-half; season with salt and pepper. Simmer for 5 minutes; do not boil. Spoon into soup bowls; garnish with pumpkin seeds and green onions.

Tomi Lessaris, Greenwood, IN

Harvest Ham Chowder

This recipe is one that all of my family really likes...it's simple enough for my daughters, Kaci, Lissi and Abbie, to make by themselves! Serve with crusty bread, crackers or cornbread.

Serves 6 to 8

2 T. oil
2 onions, diced
2 t. garlic, minced
1 green pepper, diced
4 potatoes, peeled and cubed
2 c. ham, cubed
1-1/2 to 2 c. frozen mixed vegetables
1 t. dried thyme
1 t. dried sage
salt and pepper to taste
4 to 6 c. water
2 12-oz. cans evaporated milk
1/4 c. butter, sliced
8-oz. pkg. favorite shredded cheese

Heat oil in a Dutch oven over medium-high heat; add onions, garlic, green pepper and potatoes. Sauté until onions are golden and potatoes are tender. Stir in ham, frozen vegetables and seasonings; add just enough water to cover. Bring to a boil; lower heat and simmer for 15 minutes. Add evaporated milk, butter and cheese; cover and remove from heat. Let stand 5 minutes, until butter and cheese have melted.

Pumpkin Chowder

Tara Pieron, Farmington, MI

Chicken Minestrone

This soup is just as good with other types of pasta. Use your family's favorite!

Makes 6 servings

5 10-1/2 oz. cans chicken broth
1 T. tomato paste
1-1/2 t. hot pepper sauce
1 t. dried oregano
1/2 t. dried rosemary
1-1/2 c. butternut squash, peeled
   and diced
1 T. butter
1 T. oil
1 onion, diced
3 tomatoes, chopped
1/2 lb. spinach, chopped
15-oz. can chickpeas
1 c. fresh basil, sliced
2 cloves garlic, minced
2 c. chicken, cooked and diced
6-oz. pkg. bowtie pasta, cooked

Bring broth to a boil in a large stockpot; add tomato paste, hot sauce, oregano and rosemary. Stir in squash and cook for 10 minutes; set aside. Heat butter and oil in a skillet; add onion and sauté for 4 minutes. Stir in tomatoes and heat for 3 minutes; spoon into broth mixture. Stir in spinach and chickpeas; cook for about 10 minutes. Stir in basil, garlic, chicken and pasta; heat through.

Janet Allen, Hauser, ID

Herbed Chicken-Barley Soup

Mmm...there's nothing better than homemade chicken soup! As soon as the temperature dips below freezing, I get out my big blue enamelware soup kettle and get a pot of this soup simmering.

Serves 6 to 8

3 to 4 lbs. chicken
8 c. water
1-1/2 c. carrots, diced
1 c. celery, diced
1/2 c. onion, chopped
1/2 c. pearled barley, uncooked
1 cube chicken bouillon
1/2 t. poultry seasoning
1/2 t. dried sage
1 t. salt
1/2 t. pepper
1 bay leaf

Place chicken and water in a large soup kettle. Simmer over medium heat until chicken is tender and juices run clear, about 25 to 40 minutes. Remove chicken and cool slightly, reserving broth in kettle. Allow broth to cool; skim off fat. When chicken is cool, cut into bite-size pieces, discarding bones and skin. Return chicken to broth in kettle along with remaining ingredients. Cover; simmer over low heat for at least one hour, until vegetables and barley are tender. Discard bay leaf before serving.

Chicken Minestrone

Mary Lou Wincek, South Bend, IN

Stuffed Pepper Soup

Make a double batch of this for game day. It keeps perfectly in a slow cooker on low setting all during the big game!

Serves 8 to 10

2 lbs. ground beef, browned and drained
8 c. water
28-oz. can diced tomatoes
28-oz. can tomato sauce
2 c. cooked long-grain rice
2 c. green peppers, chopped
2 cubes beef bouillon
1/4 c. brown sugar, packed
2 t. salt
1 t. pepper

Mix together all ingredients in a stockpot; bring to a boil over medium heat. Reduce heat and simmer for 30 to 40 minutes, until green peppers are tender.

Karen Augustsson, Frederick, MD

Meal-in-a-Bowl Soup

My mom was feeding a family of eight...3 girls and 3 boys, plus herself and Dad, so she would often double this recipe to accommodate all of us for dinner. You'll want to serve it with piping-hot cornbread like she did.

Makes 6 servings

6 c. chicken broth
1 c. carrot, peeled and sliced
1 c. celery, sliced
1 c. frozen corn
1 c. frozen peas
1 c. cooked elbow macaroni or small soup pasta
2 c. cooked chicken, diced
salt and pepper to taste
1 to 2 T. fresh parsley, chopped

Pour broth into a large stockpot over medium heat; bring to a simmer. Add carrot and celery; cook until crisp-tender. Reduce heat; add remaining ingredients and simmer for approximately 30 minutes.

Stuffed Pepper Soup

Roseann Papadatos, Copiaque, NY

Artichoke Pasta Salad

Take this to your next potluck...
it'll be a big hit!

Serves 6 to 8

1-lb. pkg. corkscrew pasta,
   uncooked
7-oz. jar sliced red peppers,
   drained
6-oz. jar marinated artichokes,
   drained
8-oz. jar black olives, drained
15 slices pepperoni
1/2 lb. Cheddar cheese, cubed
salt and pepper to taste
1 T. oil

Cook pasta according to package
directions, al dente but not soft.
Drain and rinse in cold water. Add
the next 5 ingredients and toss
gently. Add salt and pepper to taste;
add oil. Let marinate 2 to 4 hours.

Isolda Crockett, Mossville, IL

Big Butterflies & Mushrooms

Tastes just as good served warm
as chilled.

Makes 6 servings

1/2 c. butter
5 shallots, chopped
1-1/2 lbs. mushrooms, chopped
1/2 c. chicken broth
1/2 t. salt
1/4 t. cayenne pepper
16-oz. pkg. large bowtie pasta, cooked
1/2 c. grated Romano cheese

Melt butter in a skillet over medium
heat. Add shallots and cook until
soft. Add mushrooms and broth to
skillet. Lower heat and simmer for
4 to 5 minutes, stirring often. Add
seasonings; stir well and cook for
5 more minutes. Place cooked pasta
in a warmed large serving bowl; add
cheese and toss. Pour mushroom
sauce over pasta and gently toss to
coat well. Serve warm or chilled.

★ TIME-SAVING SHORTCUT ★ For hearty
salads in a snap, keep cans and jars of diced tomatoes,
black olives and marinated artichokes in the fridge.
They'll be chilled and ready to toss with fresh greens
and cooked rice or pasta at a moment's notice.

Artichoke Pasta Salad

Megan Brooks, Antioch, TN

Jambo

Not quite gumbo and not quite jambalaya, this dish is great with cornbread.

Makes 4 servings

3 c. Kielbasa sausage, thinly sliced
28-oz. can diced tomatoes
3 c. water
2 zucchini, halved and sliced
1/2 c. okra, sliced
1/2 c. green beans, cut into 2-inch pieces
2 bay leaves
hot pepper sauce to taste
3 to 4 c. cooked rice

Brown sausage. Combine all ingredients except hot pepper sauce and rice in a stockpot; bring to a boil. Reduce heat and simmer 20 to 25 minutes; remove and discard bay leaves. Add hot pepper sauce to taste; serve over cooked rice.

Karen Pilcher, Burleson, TX

Pork & Sauerkraut Stew

This stew conjures up warm and comforting memories of growing up in the Midwest. It has a really good flavor and the meat is so tender.

Makes 6 servings

2 14-oz. cans sauerkraut, drained
3 lbs. country-style pork ribs
4 c. cabbage, shredded
2 c. onion, coarsely chopped
2 T. brown sugar, packed
2 T. Worcestershire sauce
1-1/2 oz. pkg. onion soup mix
1 t. caraway seed
1-1/2 c. water
1-1/2 lbs. redskin potatoes, peeled and sliced

Spread sauerkraut in a large Dutch oven; add pork, cabbage and onion. Set aside. In a medium bowl, stir together remaining ingredients except potatoes; add to Dutch oven. Bring to a boil over medium-high heat; reduce heat and simmer for 2-1/2 hours, stirring occasionally. Add potatoes; cover and continue to simmer until potatoes are tender, about one hour.

Jambo

Chris Overly, Greensboro, NC

Luke's Tortellini Salad

This pasta salad is easy, delicious and colorful.

Makes 4 servings

16-oz. pkg. refrigerated cheese
   tortellini, uncooked
2 green peppers, chopped
2 c. cherry tomatoes, halved
6-oz. can sliced black olives,
   drained
light Italian salad dressing to taste
1 c. grated Parmesan cheese

Cook tortellini according to package directions; drain and rinse with cold water. Transfer tortellini to a glass bowl; refrigerate until cooled. Mix in peppers, tomatoes and olives. Just before serving time, stir in salad dressing and cheese.

Kathy Majeski, Pittsburgh, PA

Creamy Tomato Tortellini Soup

My husband Rich and I celebrate Christmas with dear friends by having a progressive dinner. When it was my turn to do the soup course a few years ago, I experimented with tomato soup recipes for a few weeks before our dinner and this was the result. We love it...and everyone always wants the recipe!

Serves 8 to 10

4 10-3/4 oz. cans tomato soup
4-1/3 c. water
14-1/2 oz. can petite diced tomatoes
1 T. fresh basil, finely chopped, or
   1 t. dried basil
Optional: salt and pepper to taste
1/2 c. fat-free half-and-half
16-oz. pkg. frozen cheese tortellini,
   cooked

In a large soup pot over medium heat, combine soup, water, tomatoes with juice and seasonings. Stir until well blended; bring to a simmer. Reduce heat and simmer 20 to 30 minutes. Stir in half-and-half; simmer over low heat an additional 5 minutes. Add cooked tortellini and heat through.

Luke's Tortellini Salad

Susan Brees, Lincoln, NE

Tuna Seashell Salad

I took this yummy salad to a potluck party and it won 1st place!

Serves 6 to 8

16-oz. pkg. shell macaroni, cooked
12-oz. can tuna, drained
3 eggs, hard-boiled, peeled and diced
4-oz. pkg. mild Cheddar cheese, diced
1/2 to 1 c. mayonnaise-type salad
    dressing
1/4 c. sweet pickle relish

Rinse macaroni with cold water; drain well. Combine all ingredients in a large serving bowl; chill.

Mary Gage, Wakewood, CA

Beefy Noodle Soup

A hearty stew-like soup...just add a basket of biscuits and dinner is served.

Serves 6 to 8

1 lb. stew beef cubes
1/2 onion, chopped
1 to 2 T. oil
2 14-1/2 oz. cans Italian-style stewed
    tomatoes
2 10-1/2 oz. cans beef broth
16-oz. pkg. frozen mixed vegetables
1 t. dried oregano
1/2 t. salt
1/4 t. pepper
1 c. medium egg noodles, uncooked

In a Dutch oven over medium-high heat, brown beef and onion in oil; drain. Add remaining ingredients except noodles. Bring to a boil; stir in noodles. Reduce heat to medium-low; cover and cook for 10 to 15 minutes, until noodles are tender.

★ TIME-SAVING SHORTCUT ★ For chilled salads, cook pasta for the shortest time given on the package, then rinse with cold water. Drain well... no mushy macaroni!

Tuna Seashell Salad

Jennifer Eveland-Kupp, Temple, PA

Fajita & Bowties Salad Bowl

Try cheddar or ranch-flavored tortilla chips...they add extra flavor to this salad!

Makes 4 servings

1/4 c. lime juice
1 T. ground cumin
1/2 t. chili powder
1/2 c. fresh cilantro, chopped
1/2 c. olive oil
15-oz. can black beans, drained and rinsed
11-oz. can corn, drained
1 c. salsa
2 tomatoes, chopped
8-oz. pkg. bowtie pasta, cooked
2 c. tortilla chips, crushed
1 c. shredded Cheddar cheese

Combine lime juice and spices in a food processor or blender. Process until almost smooth; drizzle in oil and process until blended. Set aside. In a large bowl, combine beans, corn, salsa, tomatoes, pasta and lime juice mixture; toss to combine. Gently mix in tortilla chips and cheese.

Jane Hebert, Smithfield, RI

Hearty Beef, Barley & Kale Soup

This is my friend Josephine's most favorite soup...sure to become one of your favorites too!

Serves 4 to 6

1 T. oil
1 lb. lean boneless beef, diced
2/3 to 1 c. onion, chopped
6 c. beef broth
2 c. carrots, peeled and diced
1/2 c. pearled barley, uncooked
1 t. dried thyme
Optional: 1/2 t. salt
1 lb. kale, trimmed and chopped
8-oz. pkg. sliced mushrooms

Heat oil in a large heavy soup pot over medium-high heat. Add beef and onion; cook until beef is well browned. Drain; add broth, carrots, barley, thyme and salt, if using. Bring to a boil. Reduce heat; cover and simmer for one hour, or until beef and barley are tender. Meanwhile, in a steamer basket over boiling water, steam kale for 5 minutes, until bright green; drain. Add kale and mushrooms to soup pot; return to a boil. Reduce heat; cover and simmer for another 5 to 10 minutes, until kale and mushrooms are tender.

Fajita & Bowties Salad Bowl

Ronda Sierra, Anaheim, CA

BLT Pasta Salad

We just love this salad with all the flavors of our favorite sandwich.

Makes 10 servings

8-oz. pkg. elbow macaroni, uncooked

4 c. tomatoes, peeled and chopped

4 slices bacon, crisply cooked and crumbled

3 c. shredded lettuce

1/2 c. mayonnaise

1/3 c. sour cream

1 T. Dijon mustard

1 t. sugar

2 t. cider vinegar

1/2 t. salt

1/2 t. pepper

Cook macaroni according to package directions; drain and rinse in cold water. Pour into a serving bowl. Add tomatoes, bacon and lettuce; toss gently and set aside. Mix remaining ingredients together in a mixing bowl; stir well. Pour over macaroni mixture; gently toss until well coated. Serve immediately.

★ SIMPLE INGREDIENT SWAP ★ Pasta salad is so versatile and works well with just about any veggies on hand. Toss chopped celery, cucumbers, grated carrots or even cheese chunks in for a new dish every time.

BLT Pasta Salad

Angie Cornelius, Sheridan, IL

Summer in a Bowl

We have a large, wonderful vegetable garden every summer. This salad makes excellent use of all those peppers, cucumbers and tomatoes.

Makes 4 servings

4 roma tomatoes, seeded and
  chopped
1 cubanelle pepper, seeded
  and chopped
1 cucumber, chopped
1/4 c. red onion, minced
6 fresh basil leaves, shredded
salt and pepper to taste
4 c. Italian bread, sliced, cubed
  and toasted
3 T. olive oil

Combine vegetables, basil, salt and pepper in a bowl. Let stand at room temperature for 30 minutes. At serving time, stir in bread cubes; drizzle with oil. Mix thoroughly; serve at room temperature.

Jason Keller, Carrollton, GA

Farmers' Market Soup

We just love this veggie-packed soup! Sometimes I'll use quick-cooking barley instead of noodles, adding it at the same time as the fresh veggies.

Makes 6 servings

2 c. cabbage, chopped
1 c. tomatoes, chopped
1/2 c. onion, chopped
1 c. zucchini or yellow squash,
  chopped
2 c. tomato juice
1 c. water
2 cubes beef bouillon
1 t. chili powder
1/2 t. celery seed
salt and pepper to taste
1 c. Kielbasa sausage, sliced and
  browned
1 c. thin egg noodles, cooked

In a stockpot over medium heat, combine all ingredients except sausage and noodles. Bring to a boil; reduce heat. Simmer, covered, for 45 minutes to one hour, until vegetables are tender. Add more juice or water, as needed. Stir in sausage and cooked noodles; heat through before serving.

Summer in a Bowl

Sister Toni Spencer, Watertown, SD

Sunflower Strawberry Salad

A great chilled salad...super for hot summer days!

Makes 6 servings

2 c. strawberries, hulled and sliced
1 apple, cored and diced
1 c. seedless green grapes, halved
1/2 c. celery, thinly sliced
1/4 c. raisins
1/2 c. strawberry yogurt
2 T. sunflower kernels
Optional: lettuce leaves

In a large bowl, combine fruit, celery and raisins. Stir in yogurt. Cover and chill one hour. Sprinkle with sunflower kernels just before serving. Spoon over lettuce leaves, if desired.

★ LOW-CAL ADD-ON ★ Add flavor to any salad by adding fresh, chopped herbs such as mint, parsley, dill or basil.

Lucy Davis, Colorado Springs, CO

Lucy's Sausage Salad

This deliciously different salad may be made ahead and chilled for one to two hours, or served immediately.

Makes 4 servings

14-oz. pkg. mini smoked beef
    sausages, divided
1 t. canola oil
1 c. corn
15-1/2 oz. can black beans, drained
    and rinsed
1 T. canned jalapeño pepper, seeded
    and minced
1 c. red pepper, chopped
Garnish: fresh cilantro sprigs

Measure out half the sausages; set aside for a future use. Slice remaining sausages into 3 pieces each. In a skillet, sauté sausages in oil over medium heat until lightly golden; drain. In a large bowl, combine corn, beans, jalapeño and red pepper. Stir in sausage. Toss with Dressing; garnish with cilantro.

Dressing:

3 T. low-fat plain yogurt
3 T. low-fat sour cream
1/4 c. picante sauce
1/2 c. fresh cilantro, chopped
salt and pepper to taste

Whisk together all ingredients.

Sunflower Strawberry Salad

Evelyn Belcher, Monroeton, PA

The Best Chicken Noodle Soup

My daughter gave me this recipe years ago...now it's my favorite!

Serves 8 to 10

16-oz. pkg. thin egg noodles, uncooked
12 c. chicken broth
1-1/2 T. salt
1 t. poultry seasoning
1 c. celery, chopped
1 c. onion, chopped
1 c. carrot, peeled and chopped
1/3 c. cornstarch
1/4 c. cold water
4 c. cooked chicken, diced

Cook noodles according to package directions; drain and set aside. Meanwhile, combine broth, salt and poultry seasoning in a very large pot; bring to a boil over medium heat. Stir in vegetables; reduce heat, cover and simmer for 15 minutes, or until vegetables are tender. Combine cornstarch with cold water in a small bowl; gradually add to soup, stirring constantly until thickened. Stir in chicken and noodles; heat through, about 5 to 10 minutes.

Jennie Gist, Gooseberry Patch

Lucky Noodle Bowl

We love this for a quick lunch or simple supper.

Makes 2 servings

2 c. water
3/4 c. vegetables like mushrooms, peas and spinach, finely chopped or shredded
3/4 c. cooked chicken, chopped
3-oz. pkg. chicken-flavored ramen noodles
Optional: soy sauce

In a saucepan over medium heat, bring water, vegetables and chicken to a boil. Add unbroken noodles; set aside seasoning packet. Cook for 3 minutes, until noodles are tender, turning over once or twice with a spoon so they will cook evenly. Remove pan from heat; stir in reserved seasoning. Season to taste with soy sauce, if desired.

The Best Chicken Noodle Soup

Jenny Young, Mansfield, OH

Chili-Cornbread Salad

Want a potluck salad that everyone will love? This is it! When sweet corn is in season, use it instead of the canned corn for even more flavor.

Makes 12 servings

8-1/2 oz. pkg. cornbread muffin mix
4-oz. can chopped green chiles
1/8 t. ground cumin
1/8 t. dried oregano
1/8 t. dried sage
1 c. mayonnaise
1 c. sour cream
1-oz. env. ranch salad dressing mix
2 15-oz. cans pinto beans, drained
2 15-1/2 oz. cans corn, drained
3 tomatoes, chopped
1 c. green pepper, chopped
1 c. onion, chopped
10 slices bacon, crisply cooked and crumbled
2 c. shredded Cheddar cheese

Prepare cornbread mix according to package directions; stir in chiles and seasonings. Spread batter in a greased 8"x8" baking pan. Bake at 400 degrees for 20 to 25 minutes, until center tests done; set aside to cool. In a small bowl, combine mayonnaise, sour cream and ranch dressing mix; set aside. Crumble half of the cornbread into a lightly greased glass bowl. Layer with half each of beans, mayonnaise mixture, corn, tomatoes, green pepper, onion, bacon and cheese. Repeat layers. Cover and refrigerate for 2 hours.

★ HOT TIP ★ For cornbread with a crisp, golden crust, bake it in a vintage sectioned cast-iron skillet.

Chili-Cornbread Salad

Teri Lindquist, Gurnee, IL

Italian Salad Bowl

One day I was trying to come up with a new salad to go with our spaghetti for dinner. This salad was a hit with my family...it seems everyone has a favorite ingredient in it! Feel free to add any fresh herbs from your garden.

Makes 6 servings

2 c. cherry tomatoes
1/2 lb. bite-size mozzarella cheese balls, drained
1 cucumber, peeled, halved lengthwise and sliced into half-moons
2 6-oz. jars marinated artichoke hearts, drained
6-oz. can black olives, drained
6-oz. pkg. turkey pepperoni slices
1 c. fat-free Italian salad dressing
Optional: chopped fresh oregano, parsley and/or other herbs

Combine all ingredients in a large bowl; toss gently. Cover and refrigerate about 2 hours before serving to allow flavors to blend.

Marla Caldwell, Forest, IN

Chicken Noodle Bowl

This is a great fast-fix midweek meal! It takes just thirty minutes total cooking time.

Makes 4 servings

8-oz. pkg. linguine pasta, uncooked
3 c. frozen broccoli cuts
2 carrots, peeled and sliced
2 t. oil
1 lb. boneless, skinless chicken breasts, cut into strips
1/2 c. zesty Italian salad dressing
1/3 c. teriyaki sauce
1 t. ground ginger

Cook pasta as package directs; add broccoli and carrots to the cooking water for last 2 minutes of cooking time. Drain pasta mixture. Meanwhile, heat oil in a large skillet over medium heat. Add chicken; cook until golden on all sides, stirring occasionally. Stir in remaining ingredients; cook until sauce thickens, stirring occasionally. Add pasta mixture to skillet. Stir until coated with sauce. Serve in individual bowls. Serve warm or chilled.

Italian Salad Bowl

Almine Gardner, Newport, OR

11-Layer Garden in a Bowl

This farm-fresh salad is for those occasions when seven layers just won't do!

Makes 8 servings

3 c. mayonnaise
2/3 c. sugar
2 10-oz. pkgs. mixed salad greens, divided
1 lb. bacon, crisply cooked and crumbled
1 red onion, diced
10-oz. pkg. frozen peas, thawed
1 green pepper, diced
2 c. cauliflower flowerets
2 c. broccoli flowerets
1 c. sliced mushrooms
1 c. shredded Cheddar cheese
1 c. cherry tomatoes, halved
1 T. Italian seasoning

In a bowl, mix mayonnaise and sugar until blended; set aside. Layer half the salad greens in a glass bowl. Layer with half the mayonnaise mixture, and half of each remaining ingredient except tomatoes and seasoning. Repeat layers. Top with tomatoes and sprinkle with seasoning. Cover and refrigerate 2 hours before serving.

★ HOT TIP ★ Here's a quick tip for bacon. Arrange slices on a baking sheet and bake at 350 degrees. It'll be crispy in about 15 minutes... no messy spatters!

11-Layer Garden in a Bowl

Tena Hammond Graham, Evans, GA

Tena's Delicious Gumbo

This is so easy and delicious! If you prefer, substitute the broth the chicken was simmered in.

Serves 10 to 12

4 14-1/2 oz. cans chicken broth
7-oz. pkg. gumbo mix with rice
5 to 6 boneless, skinless chicken
   breasts, cooked and chopped
1 lb. Polish sausage, cut into bite-size
   pieces
2 10-oz. pkgs. frozen chopped okra
1 green pepper, chopped
1 red pepper, chopped
1 onion, chopped
pepper to taste
Cajun seasoning to taste
2 14-oz. pkgs. frozen popcorn shrimp

Combine all ingredients except shrimp in a large stockpot. Bring to a boil; reduce heat, cover and simmer for 25 minutes. Add shrimp; simmer an additional 5 to 10 minutes.

Arlene Clifton, Toano, VA

Cream of Vegetable Soup

This wonderful soup recipe uses all the delicious vegetables available when the summer crops start to come in.

Makes 4 servings

3/4 c. butter
3/4 c. onion, diced
1-1/2 c. potatoes, peeled and diced
3/4 c. tomato, diced
3/4 c. carrot, peeled and diced
3/4 c. green beans, diced
3/4 c. broccoli, coarsely chopped
3/4 c. leek, minced
3/4 c. zucchini, minced
1 clove garlic, minced
1-1/2 t. sugar, or to taste
salt and pepper to taste
6 c. chicken broth
1/2 c. whipping cream
Garnish: chopped fresh parsley

Melt butter in a large soup pot over medium heat. Add onion and sauté until tender, 5 to 10 minutes. Reduce heat and add remaining ingredients except cream and garnish. Cover and cook until vegetables are tender, about 20 to 25 minutes. Bring to a boil. Reduce heat to low; cover and simmer 10 minutes. Let cool slightly. With an immersion blender, process soup until smooth. Increase heat to medium; gradually stir in cream. Heat through without boiling. Garnish with parsley.

Tena's Delicious Gumbo

Sally Bourdlaies, Bay City, MI

Reuben Tossed Salad

This salad was always a big hit at our son's scouting banquets. When I'm short on time, I pick up ingredients from the grocery store's salad bar and add bottles of Thousand Island salad dressing.

Serves 6 to 8

27-oz. can sauerkraut, drained
   and rinsed
1 c. carrots, peeled and grated
1 c. green pepper, chopped
8-oz. pkg. sliced Swiss cheese,
   cut into thin strips
8-oz. pkg. deli corned beef,
   thinly sliced and cut into thin
   strips
2 slices rye bread, toasted,
   buttered and cubed

In a large bowl, mix together all ingredients; toss with Dressing.

Dressing:
1/2 c. mayonnaise
2 t. chili sauce
1 T. milk
onion to taste, chopped

Combine all ingredients in a small bowl; mix well.

★ SIMPLE INGREDIENT SWAP ★
Homemade croutons absorb dressing much better than store-bought. Make your own easily by cubing bread and sprinkling them with Italian seasoning and olive oil. Toast on a baking sheet at 350 degrees for 8 to 10 minutes, until crisp.

Reuben Tossed Salad

Summer Veggie Rice Bowls, Page 116

CHAPTER THREE

Great Grains & More Bowls

Fried Chicken Bowls, Page 126

Turkey & Brown Rice Bowls, Page 108

Carla Pfall, Philadelphia, PA

Grilled Chicken Tzatziki Bowls

I've served this with grilled steak and pork as well, whatever I happen to have on hand.

Makes 4 servings

1/4 c. plain Greek yogurt
2 T. olive oil, divided
1 T. plus 1-1/2 t. red wine vinegar, divided
2 cloves garlic, minced
1/2 t. dried oregano
1 lb. boneless, skinless chicken breasts, cut into one-inch cubes
3/4 t. salt
1/4 t. pepper
3 cucumbers, thinly sliced
1 c. cherry tomatoes, halved
1/4 red onion, thinly sliced
2 c. cooked quinoa, warmed
1 c. tzatziki sauce
Garnish: sliced black olives, crumbled feta cheese

In a large bowl, whisk together yogurt, one tablespoon oil, 1-1/2 teaspoons vinegar, garlic and oregano. Add chicken; stir to coat. Cover and refrigerate for one hour. Drain chicken, discarding marinade. Thread chicken pieces onto 4 skewers. Season with salt and pepper. Grill chicken over medium-high heat, turning skewers occasionally, until golden and cooked through; set aside. In a separate bowl, whisk together remaining oil and vinegar. Add cucumbers, tomatoes and onion; toss to combine. To serve, divide quinoa among 4 bowls. Top with cucumber mixture and tzatziki sauce. Garnish as desired; top each bowl with one chicken skewer

★ STORE IT ★ Fresh tzatziki sauce is easy to make! In a medium bowl, whisk together 1 cup plain Greek yogurt; 1 cucumber, seeded, finely grated and drained; 2 cloves minced garlic; 1 teaspoon lemon zest; 1 tablespoon fresh lemon juice and 2 tablespoons chopped, fresh dill. Season with salt and pepper. Chill until ready to serve.

Grilled Chicken Tzatziki Bowls

Gaynor Simmons, Hemet, CA

Spanish-Style Round Steak

Thirty-five years ago when my children were little, I put this together with what I had in my pantry. They still request it!

Serves 6 to 8

1-1/2 lbs. beef round steak or stew
   beef, cubed
2 T. olive oil
1/2 c. onion, chopped
1 clove garlic, minced
12-oz. can cocktail vegetable juice
10-1/2 oz. can beef broth
1-1/2 c. water
1-1/2 t. salt
1/4 t. pepper
1-1/2 c. long-cooking rice, uncooked
10-oz. pkg. frozen peas
1/4 c. chopped pimentos, drained

In a skillet over medium heat, brown beef in oil. Add onion and garlic; cook and stir until onion is tender. Drain; stir in vegetable juice, broth, water, salt and pepper. Bring to a boil. Cover; reduce heat and simmer 30 minutes. Add rice, peas and pimentos. Return to a boil. Cover; reduce heat and simmer an additional 20 minutes, or until rice is tender.

Melanie Lowe, Dover, DE

Steak & Mushroom Packets

The steak strips will be much easier to cut if you freeze the meat for about 15 minutes first.

Makes 4 servings

1 lb. boneless round steak, cut into
   thin strips
1/2 t. garlic powder
1/2 t. pepper
12-oz. pkg. sliced mushrooms
1/2 c. teriyaki sauce
1/2 c. green onions, sliced
cooked rice or noodles

Sprinkle steak strips with garlic powder and pepper; place in a large plastic zipping bag. Add mushrooms and teriyaki sauce; mix well. Seal and refrigerate 2 to 4 hours. Divide steak mixture among 4 squares of aluminum foil; top with green onions. Bring up aluminum foil around ingredients; seal packets tightly. Place on a baking sheet; bake at 350 degrees for 12 to 15 minutes. Serve over cooked rice or noodles.

Spanish-Style Round Steak

JoAnn, Gooseberry Patch

Mexican Black Bean Burrito Bowls

This budget-friendly recipe is easy to double for a crowd.

Makes 4 servings

2 c. brown rice, uncooked
15-1/2 oz. can black beans, drained and rinsed
1/4 c. water
1/2 t. chili powder
1/4 t. ground cumin
1/2 t. salt, divided
1 T. olive oil
1 c. corn
1 T. fresh lime juice, divided
1/4 c. fresh cilantro, chopped and divided
4 c. romaine lettuce, finely chopped
1 c. crumbled queso blanco or feta cheese
2 avocados, peeled, pitted and sliced
1/2 c. favorite salsa
1/4 c. sour cream

Cook rice according to package directions; set aside. Meanwhile, in a saucepan over medium heat, combine beans, water, spices and 1/4 teaspoon salt; cook until heated through. Cover and remove from heat. Heat oil in a skillet over medium-high heat; add corn and cook for about 5 minutes. Sprinkle with remaining salt and one teaspoon lime juice; set aside. Transfer cooked rice to a bowl; stir in 2 tablespoons cilantro and remaining lime juice. To serve, divide beans, corn, rice, lettuce, cheese and avocado among 4 bowls. Top with salsa, sour cream and remaining cilantro.

★ SPICY SECRET ★ It's easy to make homemade salsa to serve with crispy tortilla chips or spoon over burrito bowls. Pour a 15-ounce can of stewed tomatoes, several slices of canned jalapeños and a teaspoon or two of the jalapeño juice into a blender. Cover and process to the desired consistency.

Mexican Black Bean Burrito Bowls

Sharon Tillman, Hampton, VA

Sam's Sweet-and-Sour Pork

My best friend Samantha shared this with me. A tasty dish that cooks up in a snap!

Serves 6 to 8

1 T. oil
1 lb. boneless pork loin, cut into
 1/2-inch cubes
1 c. onion, chopped
1 c. green pepper, cut into 3/4-inch
 cubes
1 c. red pepper, cut into 3/4-inch
 cubes
1 t. garlic, minced
8-oz. can pineapple chunks, drained
1 c. catsup
1 T. brown sugar, packed
1 T. white vinegar
1/2 t. salt
1/4 t. pepper
cooked rice

Heat oil in a large skillet over medium heat; brown pork on both sides. Add onion, peppers and garlic; cook and stir 5 minutes. Drain; add remaining ingredients except rice. Cover and simmer 10 minutes, or until pork is tender. Serve over hot rice.

Megan Brooks, Antioch, TN

Cornbread-Topped BBQ Beef

My sister shared this recipe with me and it has quickly become a family favorite. Not only is it super-easy to make, it's a good chance for me to sneak in some veggies for my picky eaters!

Serves 8 to 10

2 lbs. ground beef
1 onion, diced
1 green pepper, diced
11-oz. can corn, drained
14-1/2 oz. can diced tomatoes,
 drained
1/2 c. barbecue sauce
3 8-1/2 oz. pkgs. cornbread mix

In a skillet over medium heat, brown beef and onion; drain. Add vegetables; cook and stir until tender. Stir in sauce; spread mixture in an ungreased 13"x9" baking pan. Prepare cornbread according to package directions; spread batter over beef mixture. Bake, uncovered, at 400 degrees for 20 to 25 minutes, until golden and a knife tip inserted in the center comes out clean.

Sam's Sweet-and-Sour Pork

Maria Gomez, El Paso, TX

Shrimp & Bean Burrito Bowls

We often serve this with warm tortillas and extra chili sauce.

Makes 4 servings

3/4 c. chicken broth
2 15-1/2 oz. cans kidney beans, drained and rinsed
1-1/2 T. butter
1/2 t. salt, divided
1/2 t. pepper, divided
1 lb. medium shrimp, peeled and cleaned
2 t. olive oil
1-1/2 T. sweet chili sauce
2 c. cooked brown rice, warmed
1 T. fresh cilantro, chopped
1 avocado, peeled, pitted and sliced
2 T. crumbled cotija cheese or shredded Parmesan cheese
Garnish: 4 lime wedges

In a large saucepan over medium heat, bring broth and beans to a simmer. Cook for 10 minutes, stirring occasionally. Transfer bean mixture to a bowl; add butter, 1/4 teaspoon salt and 1/4 teaspoon pepper. Mash until smooth; set aside. Sprinkle shrimp with remaining salt and pepper. Add oil to a skillet over medium heat. Add shrimp and cook for 4 minutes, turning after 2 minutes. Remove from heat; stir in chili sauce. To serve, divide bean mixture and rice among 4 bowls. Top with shrimp, cilantro and avocado; sprinkle with cheese. Serve with lime wedges.

★ TIME-SAVING SHORTCUT ★ **Keep frozen shrimp on hand for delicious meals anytime. Let it thaw overnight in the fridge, or for a quicker way, place the frozen shrimp in a colander and run ice-cold water over it. Don't thaw shrimp in the microwave, as it will get mushy.**

Shrimp & Bean Burrito Bowls

Vickie, Gooseberry Patch

Mushroom & Chicken Marsala Bowls

I love these favors, but have often swapped out the spinach for kale and the quinoa for brown rice. Whatever I've got handy!

Makes 4 servings

1 c. quinoa, uncooked, rinsed and drained
1-1/2 c. chicken broth, divided
3/4 t. salt, divided
2 T. olive oil, divided
8-oz. pkg. fresh spinach
2 T. butter, divided
1 lb. mushrooms, chopped
1/2 lb. boneless, skinless chicken breast, cubed
1/4 c. onion, chopped
4 cloves garlic, thinly sliced
1-1/2 t. dried thyme
1/2 c. dry Marsala wine or chicken broth
1/4 t. pepper
1 t. dry mustard

In a saucepan over medium-high heat, combine quinoa and 1-1/4 cups broth; bring to a boil. Stir in 1/4 teaspoon salt. Remove from heat; cover and let stand. Heat 2 teaspoons oil in a skillet over medium-high heat. Add spinach and cook for 2 to 3 minutes, until wilted; remove to a bowl and set aside. Melt one tablespoon butter in skillet; add mushrooms and cook for 7 to 8 minutes. Remove mushroom mixture to a separate bowl; set aside. Add remaining oil and chicken to skillet; cook until tender and chicken juices run clear. Add onion, garlic and thyme; sauté for 2 minutes. Add remaining 1/4 cup broth and wine or broth. Cook for 2 to 3 minutes, until liquid is cooked down by 2/3. Add remaining butter, remaining salt, pepper and mustard; cook and stir until butter melts. To serve, divide quinoa among 4 bowls; top with spinach, mushrooms and chicken mixture.

Mushroom & Chicken Marsala Bowls

Luna Cooper, Huber Heights, OH

Turkey & Brown Rice Bowls

I've eaten this delicious dish for every meal...breakfast, lunch and dinner!

Makes 4 servings

4 c. cooked brown rice
4 c. fresh baby spinach leaves
1 bunch green onions, chopped
1-1/2 t. soy sauce
1 c. low-sodium chicken broth
1 lb. deli turkey breast, sliced
1 T. toasted sesame oil
Optional: 1 T. toasted sesame seed

In a saucepan over medium heat, combine cooked rice, spinach, onions, soy sauce and broth. Stir well; cook until warmed through. To serve, spoon rice mixture into 4 bowls; top each bowl with several slices turkey. Drizzle with sesame oil and sprinkle with sesame seed, if desired.

Tracey Regnold, Lewisville, TX

Pepper Chicken

This was my mother's recipe and I have modified it to fit our family. It's a favorite at our house. This dish can be made with beef too.

Serves 4 to 5

1 onion, chopped
1 green pepper, chopped
1 to 2 cloves garlic, chopped
2 to 3 T. olive oil
4 boneless, skinless chicken breasts, cubed
1/2 to 3/4 c. white wine or chicken broth
10-3/4 oz. can cream of mushroom soup
10-3/4 oz. can golden mushroom soup
1/2 c. chicken broth
salt and pepper to taste
cooked rice or egg noodles

In a skillet over medium heat, sauté onion, green pepper and garlic in oil until onion is translucent, 2 to 3 minutes. Add chicken and cook until golden, about 3 to 4 minutes; drain. Add wine or broth and cook for one to 2 minutes. Add soups, broth, salt and pepper, stirring well to combine. Simmer over medium-low heat for about 10 minutes. Serve over hot cooked rice or noodles.

Turkey & Brown Rice Bowls

Sara Jackson, Tampa, FL

Cheesy Chicken & Broccoli Rice Bowls

This was one of the first dishes I learned how to make. It's still a favorite!

Makes 4 servings

3 c. broccoli, chopped
1 T. olive oil
1/2 lb. boneless, skinless chicken breast, cubed
1/4 t. salt
1/4 t. pepper
1/2 c. green onions, chopped
1 c. shredded mild Cheddar cheese
2 c. cooked brown rice, warmed
2 T. toasted sliced almonds

In a saucepan over medium heat, cook broccoli with a small amount of water until tender; drain and set aside. Meanwhile, heat oil in a skillet over medium-high heat. Add chicken; season with salt and pepper. Cook until tender and chicken juices run clear. Add onions and cheese; cook and stir until cheese melts. Fold in cooked rice and broccoli. Cook for one to 2 minutes, until heated through. To serve, divide among 4 bowls; top with almonds.

★ FREEZE IT ★ **Making rice for dinner? Make some extra and freeze one-cup servings in plastic zipping bags. Add veggies and warm in the microwave for a quick lunch!**

Cheesy Chicken & Broccoli Rice Bowls

GREAT GRAINS & MORE

Margaret Scoresby, Mosinee, WI

Turkey & Wild Rice Casserole

We have shared this tasty recipe with many friends over the years! It's easy to double...great for drop-in guests.

Serves 4 to 6

6-oz. pkg. long-grain & wild rice, cooked
2 c. cooked turkey, diced
10-3/4 oz. can cream of mushroom soup
6-1/2 oz. can sliced mushrooms, drained
1 c. celery, thinly sliced
1 c. red pepper, chopped

Combine all ingredients in a large bowl. Spread in a lightly greased 11"x7" baking pan. Bake, covered, at 350 degrees for 30 to 40 minutes.

Doris Wilson, Denver, IA

Chicken Cashew Casserole

This is so easy, fast to make and best of all...yummy!

Makes 6 servings

2 10-3/4 oz. cans cream of mushroom soup
2/3 c. water
2 c. cooked chicken, diced
1 c. celery
1/2 c. onion, grated
6-oz. container cashews
6-oz. can sliced water chestnuts, drained and coarsely chopped
4-oz. can sliced mushrooms, drained
2 5-oz. cans chow mein noodles

Combine all ingredients except one can noodles. Spread in a lightly greased 13"x9" baking pan. Bake, uncovered, at 350 degrees for 30 minutes. Sprinkle with remaining noodles; bake for an additional 10 minutes.

Turkey & Wild Rice Casserole

Gloria Heigh, Santa Fe, NM

Quinoa Bowls with Swiss Chard & Poached Egg

Swiss chard is my favorite green veggie, so I put it in just about everything!

Makes 2 servings

3 T. olive oil, divided
1/2 onion, chopped
1 carrot, peeled and sliced
1 bunch Swiss chard, stems chopped and leaves torn, divided
1 clove garlic, minced
1 c. sliced mushrooms
2 T. water
1 t. salt
1 c. cooked quinoa, warmed
2 t. vinegar
2 eggs
pepper to taste
2 T. fresh chives, chopped

Heat one tablespoon oil in a skillet over medium-high heat. Add onion, carrot and Swiss chard stems; cook, stirring often, until softened. Add garlic and mushrooms; cook until mushrooms are softened, adding more oil if needed. Place chard leaves on top of onion mixture; add 2 tablespoons water and salt. Cover and cook until leaves wilt, about 2 minutes; stir in quinoa. Divide mixture between 2 bowls; set aside. To a saucepan over medium heat, add vinegar and 2 inches water; bring to a simmer. Crack one egg into a saucer. Using a slotted spoon, swirl simmering water in a circle; slowly add egg. Cook until yolk is softly set. Remove with a slotted spoon and place on top of one quinoa bowl. Repeat with second egg. Drizzle each bowl with one tablespoon remaining oil; sprinkle with pepper and chives.

★ HOT TIP ★ Quinoa is a delicious grain that's cooked like rice. It has a bitter-tasting natural coating, so rinse it well before cooking. Cook up a batch to sprinkle into soups, sauces and salads.

Quinoa Bowls with Swiss Chard & Poached Egg

GREAT GRAINS & MORE

Jill Burton, Gooseberry Patch

Summer Veggie Rice Bowls

This is one of my favorite meatless meals. Sometimes I'll top it with some spicy salsa...so good!

Makes 4 servings

2 c. cooked brown rice
1 c. grape tomatoes, halved
1 c. corn
1/4 c. fresh basil, chopped
1/4 c. toasted sunflower seeds
3 T. lemon juice
1 t. salt
1/4 t. pepper
3 T. olive oil, divided
1 c. zucchini, diced
1 c. yellow squash, diced
1/4 c. grated Parmesan cheese
Optional: 4 poached eggs

In a large bowl, combined cooked rice, tomatoes, corn, basil, sunflower seeds, lemon juice and seasonings. Add one tablespoon oil; toss until well blended and set aside. To a skillet over medium-high heat, add one tablespoon olive oil, zucchini and squash. Sauté for 5 to 10 minutes, stirring occasionally. Add zucchini mixture and remaining oil to rice mixture; toss well and divide among 4 bowls. Sprinkle with cheese; top with poached eggs, if desired.

Charlene McCain, Bakersfield, CA

Inside-Out Stuffed Pepper

A quick and tasty dish for those nights when you get home late from work and everybody's hungry.

Makes 4 servings

1 green pepper, top removed
1 lb. ground beef
1 onion, chopped
1-1/2 c. cooked rice
8-oz. can tomato sauce
salt and pepper to taste

Bring a saucepan of salted water to a boil. Add green pepper and cook for 8 to 10 minutes, until tender. Drain; cool slightly and slice pepper into strips. Meanwhile, cook beef and onion in a skillet over medium heat, stirring often, until beef is browned and onion is translucent. Drain; add green pepper and cooked rice to skillet. Pour tomato sauce over skillet mixture; stir and heat through. Add salt and pepper to taste.

Summer Veggie Rice Bowls

Tania Brady, Knoxville, TN

Nutty Brown Rice Bowls

A fresh and healthy lunch or dinner that goes together in a jiffy!

Makes 4 servings

4 c. cooked brown rice
15-1/2 oz. can pinto beans, drained
  and rinsed
1/4 c. red onion, chopped
1/4 c. sliced mushrooms
1/4 c. broccoli flowerets
1/4 c. green pepper, chopped
1/4 c. red pepper, chopped
1/4 c. yellow pepper, chopped
1/4 c. toasted almonds, chopped
1/4 t. pepper
1/4 c. ranch salad dressing
1 T. olive oil

Divide cooked rice among 4 bowls. Top with beans, vegetables and almonds; season with pepper. Toss salad dressing with olive oil in a small bowl; drizzle over bowls and serve.

Robyn Binns, Crescent, IA

One-Pot Beefy Macaroni

This hearty dish is perfect for weeknights when you don't want to spend the rest of the evening cleaning up the kitchen. Everything is cooked in one pot...even the pasta!

Serves 6 to 8

2 lbs. ground beef
1 onion, chopped
3 cloves garlic, chopped
3 c. water
2 14-1/2 oz. cans diced tomatoes
2 15-oz. cans tomato sauce
2 t. soy sauce
1 T. Italian seasoning
salt and pepper to taste
2 c. elbow macaroni, uncooked

Brown beef in a stockpot over medium heat; drain. Add onion and garlic; cook for 3 to 5 minutes. Stir in water, tomatoes with juice, tomato sauce, soy sauce and seasonings. Cook for 15 minutes, stirring occasionally. Add uncooked macaroni. Cover and cook for 20 to 30 minutes, stirring several times. Remove from heat. Let stand, covered, for 15 minutes.

★ SAVVY SECRET ★ Add extra texture to fresh veggies of all kinds...use a crinkle cutter or a spiral slicer to cut them into slices and sticks.

Nutty Brown Rice Bowls

Liz Plotnick-Snay, Gooseberry Patch

Chicken & Snow Pea Stir-Fry

My husband and I are always looking for new chicken dishes. This recipe turned out delicious, especially with our own additions to it.

Makes 4 servings

1 T. reduced-sodium soy sauce
1 t. chile-garlic or curry sauce
1 T. rice vinegar
2 t. toasted sesame oil
1/2 lb. boneless, skinless chicken breast, cubed
1 T. fresh ginger, peeled and minced
3 c. snow peas, trimmed
3 green onions, chopped
3 T. unsalted cashews, broken
cooked rice
Optional: additional chile-garlic sauce

Combine sauces and vinegar in a small bowl; set aside. Heat oil in a skillet over medium-high heat. Add chicken; cook and stir until no longer pink in the center. Add ginger; cook and stir for about 30 seconds. Add snow peas and onions; cook until snow peas are just tender, about 2 to 4 minutes. Add soy sauce mixture; stir to coat well. Stir in cashews just before serving. Serve over cooked rice; top with more chile-garlic sauce, if desired.

Betty Banks, Austin, TX

Quick Chinese One-Dish Meal

My hubby thinks this easy-to-make dinner is a great fixer for the "hungries."

Makes 6 servings

2 T. olive oil
1 cooked chicken breast, cubed
2 c. frozen mixed vegetables, thawed
2 c. instant rice, cooked
2 T. light brown sugar, packed
1 t. water
soy sauce to taste

Heat oil in a large skillet over medium-high heat. Add chicken and cook about 2 to 3 minutes, until hot. Add vegetables and cooked rice. In a small bowl, mix brown sugar and water together; add to skillet. Cover skillet; reduce heat to medium and cook until heated through. Add soy sauce to taste before serving.

Chicken & Snow Pea Stir-Fry

Jill Heilman, Gilbertsville, PA

Shrimp Creole

This recipe was passed down to me from my mom, and I always serve it when I entertain...everyone loves it!

Serves 4 to 6

1/3 c. shortening
1/4 c. all-purpose flour
2 lbs. uncooked large shrimp, peeled and cleaned
1 c. hot water
2 8-oz. cans tomato sauce
1/2 c. green onion, chopped
4 cloves garlic, minced
1/2 c. fresh parsley, chopped
1/4 c. green pepper, chopped
1 slice lemon
2 T. sugar
1-1/2 t. salt
1/2 t. dried thyme
1/8 t. red pepper flakes
2 bay leaves
cooked rice

Melt shortening in a large stockpot over medium heat. Whisk in flour; cook until it starts to brown. Add remaining ingredients except cooked rice. Cover and simmer for 20 minutes. Discard bay leaves. Spoon over cooked rice.

Stacy Lane, Millsboro, DE

Chicken Lo Mein

I first learned this recipe in my home economics class in high school. I took it home, revamped it a little, and we've been enjoying it for over ten years now. You can use any meat and vegetables you have on hand. I often share the recipe with first-time cooks and newlyweds, since it's so easy to make and easy on the budget.

Makes 5 servings

1 T. oil
2 boneless, skinless chicken breasts, sliced
1 to 2 c. chopped broccoli, carrots, cabbage, celery and/or mushrooms
4 3-oz. pkgs. low-sodium chicken-flavored ramen noodles
4 c. water
1 T. low-sodium soy sauce
2 t. cornstarch
1 t. garlic powder
1 t. dried parsley
Optional: onion powder to taste

Heat oil in a large saucepan over medium heat. Add chicken; sauté until golden. Add vegetables to saucepan; break up ramen noodles and add to saucepan. In a separate saucepan, bring water to a boil. Stir in remaining ingredients, adding contents of seasoning packets to taste; add to chicken mixture. Cover and cook over medium-high heat for about 10 minutes, until vegetables are tender.

Shrimp Creole

Patty Perry, Bloomington, IN

Picture-Perfect Paella

This classic Spanish dish is amazingly delicious! If you choose not to use seafood, substitute sausage links, browning them along with the chicken.

Makes 8 servings

3 lbs. chicken thighs and/or breasts
2 onions, quartered
1 stalk celery, sliced
2 carrots, peeled and sliced
salt and pepper to taste
6 c. water
2 c. long-cooking rice, uncooked
2 cloves garlic, crushed
1/4 c. oil
1 c. frozen baby peas
1/4 c. diced pimentos, drained
1/2 t. dried oregano
1/8 t. saffron or turmeric
1 lb. uncooked large shrimp, peeled and cleaned
12 uncooked clams in shells

In a very large deep cast-iron skillet over medium heat, combine chicken, onions, celery, carrots, salt, pepper and water. Bring to a boil. Reduce heat to medium-low. Cover and simmer for one hour. Remove chicken and vegetables to a platter; reserve 6 cups of the broth in a bowl. Dice chicken and set aside, discarding bones. In the same skillet over medium heat, cook and stir rice and garlic in oil until golden. Add reserved chicken, reserved broth, peas, pimentos and herbs. Cover and cook over low heat for 15 minutes. Add shrimp and clams; cover and cook for another 10 minutes, or until shrimp turn pink and clams have opened.

★ FREEZE IT ★ Freezing extra pieces of chicken? Add a flavorful marinade to plastic zipping bags of uncooked chicken and freeze. When you thaw it for cooking, the chicken will be deliciously seasoned. So convenient!

Picture-Perfect Paella

Linda Jancik, Huron, OH

Fried Chicken Bowls

Drizzle with warm gravy for real comfort food!

Makes 4 servings

oil for frying
4 pieces frozen breaded chicken
    strips
2 c. mashed potatoes
1 c. shredded Cheddar cheese
14-oz. can corn, drained

Heat one inch oil in a saucepan to 350 degrees. Add chicken strips and cook until heated through, 2 to 3 minutes. Remove from pan; drain on a paper towel-lined plate. Cut chicken into bite-size pieces. To serve, layer warmed potatoes, cheese, warmed corn and chicken among 4 bowls.

Danielle Fish, Acworth, GA

Spicy Chicken Tenders

One night I created this dish for my husband, Ryan, and he ate his dinner so fast, he was asking for seconds! I serve it with roasted broccoli and cauliflower for a complete meal.

Serves 2 to 3

3/4 lb. boneless chicken tenders
1 T. olive oil
Optional: 1 c. sliced mushrooms
3 T. reduced-sodium soy sauce
1 to 1-1/2 t. red pepper flakes
cooked rice

In a skillet over medium-high heat, cook chicken in oil until golden. Stir in remaining ingredients except rice, adding red pepper flakes to taste. Let simmer until chicken is cooked through. Serve over cooked rice.

★ SPICY SECRET ★ Give the same ol' mashed potatoes some pizazz...stir in a tablespoon or two of horseradish sauce.

Fried Chicken Bowls

Suzanne Rutan, Auburn, NY

Black-Eyed Peas & Potato Skillet

Nothing beats the taste of freshly snipped dill from your herb garden... so zesty and bright! I love the taste of it, so I try to put it on everything I can.

Makes 2 servings

1/3 c. dried black-eyed peas
1-1/2 c. new redskin potatoes, halved
1 T. olive oil
1 red onion, diced
1 T. fresh rosemary, chopped
2 T. fresh dill, chopped
1/4 t. salt
2 eggs
Garnish: additional chopped fresh dill

Fill a large saucepan with water; bring to a boil. Add peas and cook until almost tender, about 15 to 18 minutes. Add potatoes and cook another 5 to 6 minutes, until potatoes and peas are tender. Drain and set aside. Heat oil in a large skillet over medium heat. Add onion and cook until translucent, about 4 to 5 minutes. Stir in potatoes, peas and seasonings. Cook until potatoes are golden. Make 2 wells in potato mixture and crack one egg into each well. Cover and cook until eggs reach desired doneness. Remove from heat and sprinkle with dill.

★ DOUBLE DUTY ★ Some plants belong to both herbs and spices. Dill seed is considered a spice while the plant and leaves are herbs.

Black-Eyed Peas & Potato Skillet

Charlie Tuggle, Palo Alto, CA

Chicken Enchilada Nacho Bowls

This is my wife's favorite Friday-night dinner. A tall glass of iced tea and dinner is complete!

Makes 4 servings

1 onion, diced
1 T. olive oil
10-oz. can enchilada sauce
1 c. canned crushed tomatoes
15-1/2 oz. can black beans, drained and rinsed
1 t. dried oregano
1 T. brown sugar, packed
2 c. rotisserie chicken, shredded
8-oz. pkg. tortilla or corn chips, coarsely crushed
1-1/4 c. shredded Cheddar cheese
2 c. lettuce, shredded
1/4 c. fresh cilantro, chopped
Garnish: 4 lime slices
Optional: hot pepper sauce

In a skillet over medium-high heat, sauté onion in oil until softened. Add enchilada sauce, tomatoes, beans, oregano and sugar; cook, stirring occasionally, until hot and slightly cooked down about 5 minutes. Stir in chicken; cook until warmed through. To serve, divide chips among 4 bowls; top with chicken mixture, cheese, lettuce and cilantro. Serve with lime slices and hot sauce, if desired.

Sarah Lundvall, Ephrata, PA

Quick One-Pot Burrito Bowl

This is one of those go-to meals I fix on nights when we get home late from work and want dinner quickly.

Makes 4 servings

3 T. olive oil
1/2 c. onion, chopped
1 clove garlic, minced
1 cooked chicken breast, diced
1 c. long-cooking brown rice, uncooked
14-oz. can chicken broth
14-1/2 oz. can diced tomatoes with green chiles
15-1/2 oz. can light red kidney beans, drained and rinsed
11-oz. can corn, drained
1 T. dried cumin
2 t. chili powder
1/2 t. garlic powder
1/4 t. pepper
2 c. shredded Cheddar cheese

Heat oil in a skillet over medium heat. Sauté onion and garlic until translucent. Add chicken and cook for 2 minutes. Add uncooked rice; cook and stir until lightly toasted. Stir in broth, tomatoes with juice and remaining ingredients except cheese. Bring to a boil; reduce heat to low. Cover and simmer for 25 minutes, or until liquid is mostly absorbed. Turn off heat. Uncover and sprinkle with cheese. Cover and let stand for 3 to 5 minutes, until cheese is melted.

Chicken Enchilada Nacho Bowls

David Archie, Salt Lake City, UT

Skillet Chicken with Vegetables & Herbs

A complete dinner of roast chicken and veggies...all in one pan!

Makes 4 servings

2 T. all-purpose flour
1/8 t. pepper
1/8 t. paprika
4 chicken breasts
2 T. olive oil
2 red onions, quartered
1 lb. new potatoes, quartered
8-oz. pkg. baby carrots
1-1/2 c. chicken broth
3 T. lemon juice
1 T. fresh oregano, chopped
Garnish: chopped fresh thyme

Combine flour and seasonings in a shallow bowl; coat chicken breasts well. Heat oil in a large cast-iron skillet over medium-high heat. Brown chicken on both sides. Remove chicken from skillet and set aside; reserve drippings in skillet. Add onions and potatoes to skillet; cook for 5 minutes. Add carrots, chicken broth, lemon juice and oregano; bring to a boil. Return chicken to skillet. Cover skillet and transfer to oven. Bake at 350 degrees for 20 minutes. Uncover and bake an additional 15 minutes, or until chicken juices run clear and vegetables are tender. Garnish with a sprinkle of thyme.

★ HOT TIP ★ **Grandma's good old cast-iron skillet is wonderful for cooking up one-dish dinners. If the skillet hasn't been used in awhile, season it first...rub it all over with oil, bake at 300 degrees for an hour and let it cool completely in the oven.**

Skillet Chicken with Vegetables & Herbs

Brenda Hager, Nancy, KY

Sourdough Chicken Casserole

My husband really enjoys this delicious dish, and he's not a big fan of chicken. The caramelized onions give it a great flavor!

Makes 4 servings

4 c. sourdough bread, cubed
6 T. butter, melted and divided
1/3 c. grated Parmesan cheese
2 T. fresh parsley, chopped
2 sweet onions, sliced
8-oz. pkg. sliced mushrooms
10-3/4 oz. can cream of mushroom
  soup
1 c. white wine or buttermilk
2-1/2 c. cooked chicken, shredded
1/2 c. roasted red peppers, drained
  and chopped
1/2 t. salt
1/4 t. pepper

Toss together bread cubes, 1/4 cup butter, cheese and parsley in a large bowl; set aside. Sauté onions in remaining 2 tablespoons butter in a large skillet over medium-high heat 15 minutes, or until dark golden. Add mushrooms and sauté 5 minutes. Add remaining ingredients. Cook 5 more minutes, stirring constantly, until hot and bubbly. Pour into 4 lightly greased ramekins; top each ramekin with bread cube mixture. Bake, uncovered, at 400 degrees for 15 minutes, or until golden.

★ FREEZE IT ★ Grandma never tossed out day-old bread and neither should you! It keeps its texture better than very fresh bread...it's thrifty too. Cut it into cubes, pack into freezer bags and freeze for making stuffing cubes, casserole toppings and herbed salad croutons.

Sourdough Chicken Casserole

Terri Lock, Carrollton, MO

Beef Porcupine Meatballs

As a teacher, I need fast homestyle meals to serve to my family of five before I leave for evening school events...this recipe is perfect.

Serves 4 to 6

8-oz. pkg. beef-flavored rice
  vermicelli mix
1 lb. ground beef
1 egg, beaten
2-1/2 c. water
cooked egg noodles

In a bowl, combine rice vermicelli mix, beef and egg, reserving seasoning packet from mix. Form mixture into one-inch balls. In a skillet over medium heat, cook meatballs, turning occasionally, until browned on all sides; drain. In a bowl, combine seasoning packet and water; pour over meatballs. Cover and simmer for 30 minutes, or until thickened and meatballs are no longer pink in the center. Serve meatballs and sauce over noodles.

Diane Cohen, The Woodlands, TX

Smoked Sausage Stir-Fry

This veggie-packed dish stirs up in no time at all...you'll love it!

Makes 6 servings

2 T. olive oil
14-oz. pkg. smoked pork sausage,
  thinly sliced
16-oz. pkg. frozen Asian-blend
  stir-fry vegetables
6 T. sweet-and-sour sauce
cooked rice

In a skillet, heat oil over medium-high heat. Add sausage; sauté for one minute. Add vegetables; cook and stir for 6 to 8 minutes, or until thawed and heated through. Stir in sauce; cook and stir for one additional minute, until coated. Serve over hot cooked rice.

★ TIME-SAVING SHORTCUT ★ Quick-cooking smoked sausage links are a great choice for weeknight meals. Different flavors like hickory-smoked or cheese-filled sausage can really jazz up a recipe too.

Beef Porcupine Meatballs

Lynn Ruble, Decatur, IN

Honey Chicken Stir-Fry

Measure out the seasonings before you begin to stir-fry...this dish comes together very quickly.

Serves 4 to 6

2 lbs. boneless, skinless chicken
  breasts, cut into bite-size pieces
1/4 c. honey, divided
1 egg, beaten
1/3 c. plus 1 T. water, divided
1 t. Worcestershire sauce
1/2 t. dried thyme
1/4 t. lemon-pepper seasoning
1/4 t. garlic powder
1/8 t. dried oregano
1/8 t. dried marjoram
2 T. vegetable oil
1 T. cornstarch
14-oz. pkg. frozen stir-fry vegetables
1/4 t. salt
cooked rice

In a large bowl, combine chicken, 2 tablespoons honey, egg, 1/3 cup water, Worcestershire sauce and seasonings; set aside. Heat oil in a wok or large skillet over medium-high heat. Add chicken; cook, stirring frequently, until golden. Remove chicken from wok; keep warm. In a small bowl, mix cornstarch with remaining 2 tablespoons honey and one tablespoon water; set aside. Add vegetables to wok; sprinkle with salt. Cook over medium-high heat 6 to 8 minutes, or until vegetables begin to thaw; drizzle with cornstarch mixture. Continue cooking 6 minutes, or until vegetables are tender; stir in chicken and heat through. Serve with rice.

★ SAVVY SECRET ★ Unless specified in a recipe, add mild-flavored fresh herbs like marjoram and parsley to soups and stews near the end of cooking time...they won't lose their delicate flavor.

Honey Chicken Stir-Fry

Gingery Asian Pasta Bowls, Page 146

CHAPTER FOUR

Pasta Bowls

Basil-Broccoli Pasta, Page 156

Pepperoni Tortellini, Page 162

Shari Johnson, St. Cloud, MN

Chicken Spring Roll Bowls

All the flavors of your favorite spring roll!

Makes 4 servings

12-oz. pkg. rice noodles or angel hair pasta, uncooked
1 T. olive oil
3 boneless, skinless chicken breasts
1/2 t. salt
1/4 t. pepper
4 large lettuce leaves
1 c. carrot, peeled and shredded
3 green onions, sliced
1 avocado, peeled, pitted and sliced
Garnish: chopped peanuts
Peanut Sauce

Cook noodles according to package directions; drain. Meanwhile, heat oil in a skillet over medium heat. Add chicken; season with salt and pepper. Cook until lightly golden on both sides, 8 to 10 minutes. Cool slightly; slice chicken and set aside. To serve, divide noodles among 4 bowls. Top each bowl with a lettuce leaf, 1/4 cup carrot, one tablespoon onion, 3 slices avocado and 6 slices chicken. Garnish each bowl with peanuts and 1/4 cup Peanut Sauce.

Peanut Sauce:

1/2 c. creamy peanut butter
1/2 c. water
1 T. soy sauce
1/4 t. ground ginger
1 t. brown sugar, packed
1 t. garlic, minced
1 t. rice vinegar

In a small bowl, whisk together all ingredients until smooth.

★ SPICY SECRET ★ Some like it hot! There are lots of ways to turn up the heat in familiar recipes...hot pepper sauce, creamy horseradish, hot Chinese mustard, Japanese wasabi or sriracha from Thailand. Try 'em all...see what you like!

Chicken Spring Roll Bowls

Jennifer Niemi, Nova Scotia, Canada

Rosemary Peppers & Fusilli

This colorful, flavorful meatless meal is ready to serve in a jiffy. If you can't find fusilli pasta, try medium shells, rotini or even wagon wheels.

Makes 4 servings

2 to 4 T. olive oil
2 red onions, thinly sliced and
   separated into rings
3 red, orange and/or yellow peppers,
   very thinly sliced
5 to 6 cloves garlic, very thinly sliced
3 t. dried rosemary
salt and pepper to taste
12-oz. pkg. fusilli pasta, cooked
Optional: shredded mozzarella
   cheese

Add oil to a large skillet over medium heat. Add onions to skillet; cover and cook over medium heat for 10 minutes. Stir in remaining ingredients except pasta and cheese; reduce heat. Cook, covered, stirring occasionally, for an additional 20 minutes. Serve vegetable mixture over pasta, topped with cheese if desired.

Robyn Holdsworth, Caribou, ME

Tuna Pea Doodle

This dish with the funny name always puts a smile on my three sons' faces whenever I make it.

Makes 6 servings

10-3/4 oz. can cream of mushroom soup
1-1/4 c. milk
3 T. butter, diced
16-oz. pkg. medium egg noodles, cooked
15-1/4 oz. can peas, drained
12-oz. can solid white tuna, drained
celery salt and pepper to taste

Mix together soup, milk and butter in a large saucepan over low heat. Gently stir in noodles, peas and tuna. Simmer until heated through, about 10 minutes. Stir in celery salt and pepper to taste.

★ STORE IT ★ Use dried herbs from the herb garden to make a terrific seasoning blend. Combine one cup sea salt with 2 tablespoons each of rosemary, thyme, lemon balm, mint, tarragon, dill weed and paprika. Stir in 4 tablespoons parsley and basil. Blend, in batches, in a food processor, and store in a glass shaker.

Rosemary Peppers & Fusilli

Liz Plotnick-Snay, Gooseberry Patch

Gingery Asian Pasta Bowls

This dish is so easy to make, and is ready in about 20 minutes!

Makes 4 servings

8-oz. pkg. capellini pasta, uncooked
1/2 lb. sliced mushrooms
1 red pepper, thinly sliced
1/4 c. onion, diced
1 T. oil
1 T. fresh parsley, chopped

Cook pasta according to package instructions; drain. Meanwhile, in a skillet over medium heat, sauté mushrooms, pepper and onion in oil until softened, about 5 minutes. To serve, divide pasta among 4 bowls; top with vegetables. Drizzle with Ginger Dressing; sprinkle with parsley.

Ginger Dressing:

1/4 c. rice vinegar
3 T. soy sauce
1 T. oil
1 t. fresh ginger, peeled and grated

In a small bowl, whisk together all ingredients.

Annelise Sophiea, Traverse City, MI

Annie's Winter Couscous Bowl

This recipe has become an instant winter classic in our household. The beautiful red, green and white colors make you feel right in the season. It's now a family favorite.

Serves 4 to 6

1/4 to 1/2 c. pine nuts
1 avocado, pitted, peeled and diced
2 t. lemon juice
1-1/2 c. water
1-1/2 c. couscous, uncooked and rinsed
1 cucumber, sliced
1 c. crumbled feta cheese
1/4 c. fresh cilantro, minced
seeds of 1 pomegranate
2 T. honey
1 t. cinnamon

Toast pine nuts in a dry skillet until golden; set aside. In a small bowl, mix together avocado and lemon juice; set aside. In a saucepan over high heat, bring water to a boil. Stir in couscous; cook until tender, about 10 to 15 minutes. Fluff couscous with a fork; transfer to a serving bowl. Add pine nuts, avocado mixture and remaining ingredients. Mix together thoroughly and serve.

Gingery Asian Pasta Bowls

Julie Swenson, Minneapolis, MN

Spicy Pork
Noodle Bowls

This recipe calls for pork, but I often
switch it up and use grilled chicken
or steak.

Makes 4 servings

**8-oz. pkg. linguine pasta,
   uncooked and divided**
2 T. oil, divided
**1 lb. boneless pork shoulder,
   sliced into strips**
1 onion, thinly sliced
**1/2 lb. broccoli, cut into bite-size
   flowerets**
2 T. Worcestershire sauce
1 T. soy sauce
2 t. cornstarch
1/2 t. curry powder
1 tomato, chopped

Cook half of pasta according to
package directions; set aside.
Reserve remaining pasta for another
recipe. Heat one tablespoon oil in
a large skillet over high heat. Add
pork; cook and stir until golden,
about 7 minutes. Remove pork; set
aside. Heat remaining oil in skillet;
add onion and broccoli. Cook and
stir until tender, about 5 minutes.
Mix together sauces, cornstarch
and curry powder in a cup; stir into
skillet. Cook and stir until slightly
thickened. Return pork to pan; heat
through. Divide cooked pasta into
4 shallow bowls. Top with pork
mixture and tomato; toss to
coat pasta.

★ HOT TIP ★ So many favorite comfort-food
recipes begin with pasta or noodles. The secret
to perfectly cooked pasta is to use plenty of
cooking water...about a gallon per pound of
pasta, in a very large pot.

Spicy Pork Noodle Bowls

Sheila Bane, Waynetown, IN

Creamy Fettuccine Alfredo

This has been one of my tried & true recipes for over twenty years. It's a favorite of my kids...try it and you'll agree!

Makes 6 servings

16-oz. pkg. fettuccine pasta, uncooked
1 t. salt
2/3 c. butter, softened
1-1/2 c. half-and-half, room temperature, divided
1-1/2 c. shredded Parmesan cheese
1/4 t. garlic salt
Garnish: additional shredded Parmesan cheese

Cook pasta as package directs, adding salt to cooking water. Remove pan from heat; drain pasta and return to pan. Add butter to warm pasta and mix well. Add 3/4 cup half-and-half to pasta; mix well. In a small bowl, mix together cheese and garlic salt. Add half of cheese mixture to pasta mixture. Add remaining half-and-half and remaining cheese mixture to pasta mixture, stirring well after each addition. Garnish with additional cheese and serve immediately.

Diane Cohen, The Woodlands, TX

Cheesy Chicken & Rotini

A delicious made-from-scratch meal... with no more effort than preparing a boxed dinner helper!

Makes 5 servings

2 c. rotini pasta, uncooked
1 lb. boneless, skinless chicken breasts, cut into bite-size pieces
1 green pepper, thinly sliced
16-oz. jar spaghetti sauce
8-oz. pkg. shredded Italian blend or mozzarella cheese, divided

Cook rotini according to package directions; drain. Spray a skillet with non-stick vegetable spray; heat over medium-high heat. Add chicken; cook and stir for 5 minutes. Add pepper and cook for an additional 5 minutes, until chicken is cooked through. Stir in sauce, cooked rotini and one cup cheese; sprinkle with remaining cheese. Remove from heat; cover and let stand for one to 2 minutes, until cheese is melted.

Creamy Fettuccine Alfredo

Melinda Daniels, Lewiston, ID

Melinda's Veggie Stir-Fry

I really like stir-fry and chow mein, so I created this recipe using the items that I had in my garden and fridge. It is now one of my family's favorites and makes great leftovers too.

Serves 6 to 8

8-oz. pkg. spaghetti, uncooked
2 c. broccoli, cut into bite-size
    flowerets
1 c. snow or sugar snap pea pods,
    halved
2 carrots, peeled and thinly sliced
1/2 onion, thinly sliced
1/4 green pepper, thinly sliced

Cook spaghetti as package directs; drain and set aside. Meanwhile, place vegetables into a steamer basket; place in a large stockpot filled with enough water to just reach the bottom of the basket. Heat over medium heat and steam for about 3 to 5 minutes, until just beginning to soften; drain. If crisper vegetables are desired, omit this step. When spaghetti and vegetables are done, add to Stir-Fry Sauce in skillet. Cook and stir over medium-high heat for about 15 minutes, to desired tenderness.

Stir-Fry Sauce:

1/2 c. olive oil
1/3 c. soy sauce
2 T. Dijon mustard
2 T. sliced pepperoncini, chopped
2 cloves garlic, minced
1 t. pepper

In a large skillet over low heat, mix all ingredients together. Simmer until heated through.

★ TIME-SAVING SHORTCUT ★ Stir-frying is a terrific way to make a quick and tasty dinner. Slice veggies into equal-size cubes or slices before you start cooking...they'll all be done to perfection at the same time.

Melinda's Veggie Stir-Fry

Angie Whitmore, Farmington, UT

Angie's Pasta & Sauce

Homemade sauce is so simple to prepare. You'll love the taste of both the sauce and the freshly grated Parmesan on top.

Serves 4 to 6

6 to 8 roma tomatoes, halved, seeded
    and diced
1 to 2 cloves garlic, minced
1/4 to 1/2 c. butter, melted
1 T. dried basil
8-oz. pkg. angel hair pasta, cooked
Garnish: freshly grated Parmesan
    cheese

Combine tomatoes and garlic in a saucepan. Simmer over medium heat 15 minutes; set aside. Blend together butter and basil; add to pasta. Toss to coat. Stir in tomato mixture and garnish.

Connie Hilty, Pearland, TX

Speedy Tomato Mac & Cheese

This is a snap to make and a real family pleaser. My four kids, ages four to ten, just love it...we never have any leftovers unless I make a double batch!

Serves 4 to 6

2 c. elbow macaroni, uncooked
10-3/4 oz. can Cheddar cheese soup
1 c. zesty spaghetti sauce
1/3 c. milk
Garnish: grated Parmesan cheese

Cook macaroni according to package directions; drain and return to saucepan. Add soup, sauce and milk; mix well and heat through over medium heat. Serve with Parmesan cheese.

★ PENNY PINCHER ★ **Try serving a meatless main once a week...it's economical and healthy too. There are lots of tasty pasta and rice-based dishes to choose from.**

Angie's Pasta & Sauce

Steve Fretz, San Francisco, CA

Basil-Broccoli Pasta

Serve this dish as either a yummy side or a meatless main.

Serves 4 to 6

16-oz. pkg. rigatoni pasta, uncooked
2 T. butter
6 T. olive oil
4 cloves garlic, sliced
1 bunch broccoli, sliced into flowerets
1 c. vegetable broth
pepper to taste
Garnish: chopped fresh basil, grated
   Parmesan cheese

Cook pasta according to package directions; drain. Meanwhile, melt butter with oil in a large deep cast-iron skillet over medium heat. Add garlic; cook until lightly golden. Add broccoli; increase heat to medium-high. Cook, stirring often, until broccoli is almost tender, about 3 to 4 minutes. Pour in vegetable broth; reduce heat to low. Cover and simmer until broccoli is tender. Stir cooked pasta into mixture in skillet; mix thoroughly and heat through. Season with pepper. Top with basil and Parmesan cheese.

★ SIMPLE INGREDIENT SWAP ★ **Prefer a meatless dinner salad? Substitute roasted, salted pecans for crispy bacon as a salad topping with a similar salty-smoky taste and crunch.**

Basil-Broccoli Pasta

JoAnn, Gooseberry Patch

Pepperoni-Pizza Rigatoni

Personalize this recipe by adding mushrooms, black olives or any of your family's other favorite pizza toppings.

Makes 6 servings

1-1/2 lbs. ground beef, browned and drained
8-oz. pkg. rigatoni, cooked
16-oz. pkg. shredded mozzarella cheese
10-3/4 oz. can cream of tomato soup
2 14-oz. jars pizza sauce
8-oz. pkg. sliced pepperoni

Alternate layers of ground beef, cooked rigatoni, cheese, soup, sauce and pepperoni in a slow cooker. Cover and cook on low setting for 4 hours.

Denise Webb, Galveston, IN

Denise's Penne Rosa

Creamy and delicious...this recipe always makes me feel like I'm eating at my favorite Italian restaurant!

Makes 4 servings

1 T. butter
1 T. garlic, minced
14-1/2 oz. can whole tomatoes, finely chopped, drained and 1/4 c. juice reserved
1 t. dried basil
salt and pepper to taste
2/3 c. whipping cream
8-oz. pkg. penne rigate pasta, cooked
Garnish: 2 T. grated Parmesan cheese

Melt butter in a skillet over medium heat. Add garlic and cook for one minute, until golden. Add tomatoes with reserved juice, basil, salt and pepper; heat to boiling. Reduce heat; simmer for 5 minutes, or until most of liquid is reduced. Stir in cream. Heat through on low heat for one minute, or until thickened. Toss sauce with cooked pasta; sprinkle with cheese. Serve immediately.

Pepperoni-Pizza Rigatoni

Vickie, Gooseberry Patch

Antipasto-Style Linguine

I've always been a big fan of antipasto. I love having all the same flavors over pasta.

Serves 4 to 6

12-oz. pkg. linguine pasta, uncooked
16-oz. jar antipasto salad with olives, divided
3 T. olive oil
4 portabella mushroom caps, sliced
6-oz. pkg. sliced deli salami, cut into thin strips
2 c. shredded Asiago cheese, divided
2 c. fresh basil, chopped and divided
pepper to taste

Cook pasta and drain, reserving 1/2 cup cooking water; set aside. Measure one cup antipasto salad vegetables and 6 tablespoons marinade from jar; reserve remainder for another recipe. Slice vegetables and set aside. Heat oil in pasta pot over medium-high heat. Sauté mushrooms until tender, about 6 minutes. Add salami; cook and stir briefly. Add pasta, reserved cooking water, vegetables, reserved marinade and 1-1/2 cups cheese; toss until liquid thickens and coats pasta, about 3 minutes. Stir in 1-1/2 cups basil; add pepper to taste. Garnish with remaining basil and cheese.

★ SAVVY SIDE ★ Top slices of warm bread with flavorful Basil-Tomato Butter...it's easy to make. Blend 1/2 cup softened butter with 1/3 cup shredded fresh basil, one tablespoon tomato paste and 1/4 teaspoon salt.

Antipasto-Style Linguine

Eileen Boomgaarden, Waukesha, WI

Pepperoni Tortellini

Sometimes I use green, yellow or orange peppers in this recipe. They are all so colorful and taste great!

Serves 4 to 6

2 t. olive oil
1 onion, sliced
1 red pepper, thinly sliced
3 to 4 cloves garlic, chopped
5-oz. pkg. sliced pepperoni, cut into strips
1-1/2 t. dried basil
1-1/2 t. dried oregano
1 t. Italian seasoning
1 t. garlic powder
1/2 t. salt
1/4 t. pepper
8-oz. pkg. refrigerated 3-cheese tortellini pasta, cooked
Garnish: shaved Parmesan cheese, fresh basil

Heat oil in a skillet over medium heat. Sauté onion, red pepper and garlic until crisp-tender. Add remaining ingredients except pasta and garnish. Cook, stirring occasionally, for 5 minutes. Stir in pasta and cook until heated through. Garnish with Parmesan cheese and basil.

Doris Stegner, Delaware, OH

Sunday Meatball Skillet

Oh-so delicious alongside roasted green beans and a bowl of homemade applesauce!

Makes 4 servings

1 lb. ground beef
1 c. onion, grated
1/2 c. Italian-flavored dry bread crumbs
1 egg, beaten
1/4 c. catsup
1/4 t. pepper
2 c. beef broth
1/4 c. all-purpose flour
1/2 c. sour cream
8-oz. pkg. medium egg noodles, cooked
Garnish: chopped fresh parsley

In a bowl, combine beef, onion, bread crumbs, egg, catsup and pepper. Shape into one-inch meatballs. Spray a skillet with non-stick vegetable spray. Cook meatballs over medium heat, turning occasionally, until browned, about 10 minutes. Remove meatballs and let drain on paper towels. In a bowl, whisk together broth and flour; add to skillet. Cook and stir until mixture thickens, about 5 minutes. Stir in sour cream. Add meatballs and noodles; toss to coat. Cook and stir until heated through, about 5 minutes. Garnish with parsley.

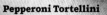
Pepperoni Tortellini

Barbara Adamson, Oviedo, FL

Bacon Florentine Fettuccine

This incredibly tasty and simple pasta dish is so fast to prepare.

Makes 4 servings

16-oz. pkg. fettuccine pasta, uncooked
2 10-oz. pkgs. frozen creamed spinach
1/2 lb. bacon, crisply cooked and crumbled
1/8 t. garlic powder
1/2 c. plus 2 T. grated Parmesan cheese, divided
pepper to taste

Prepare fettuccine in a stockpot as package directs; drain, reserving 3/4 cup of cooking liquid. Microwave spinach as directed on package. Add spinach, bacon and garlic powder to stockpot. Slowly drizzle reserved liquid into stockpot until sauce reaches desired consistency. Return pasta to stockpot and heat through. Transfer to a serving dish and stir in 1/2 cup cheese. Season with pepper; sprinkle with remaining cheese.

Katie Wollgast, Florissant, MO

Scalloped Cabbage & Ham

Packaged coleslaw mix makes this old-fashioned favorite easy... horseradish gives it a little kick! Add a basket of warm pumpernickel bread for a hearty, satisfying meal.

Makes 4 servings

2 c. cooked ham, cubed
1/2 c. long-cooking rice, uncooked
1 onion, chopped
1 T. oil
10-3/4 oz. can cream of mushroom soup
1-1/2 c. milk
1 t. prepared horseradish
1 t. salt
16-oz. pkg. coleslaw mix
Garnish: 1 T. dried parsley

In a skillet over medium heat, sauté ham, uncooked rice and onion in oil until lightly golden. Stir in remaining ingredients except parsley; bring to a boil. Reduce heat to low; cover and simmer for 20 to 25 minutes, stirring occasionally, until rice and coleslaw mix are tender. Sprinkle with parsley just before serving.

Bacon Florentine Fettuccine

Jacob Jackson, Phoenix, AZ

Zippy Ziti & Broccoli

Sometimes I add some diced rotisserie chicken from the deli for a heartier meal.

Serves 4 to 6

8-oz. pkg. ziti pasta, uncooked
2 c. frozen broccoli cuts
1 clove garlic, minced
16-oz. jar Alfredo sauce
14-1/2 oz. can Italian-style
    diced tomatoes
2 c. shredded mozzarella
    cheese
2 T. Italian-flavored dry bread
    crumbs
2 t. margarine, melted

Prepare ziti according to package directions; add broccoli during last minute of cooking time. Drain; add garlic, Alfredo sauce, tomatoes and cheese, mixing well. Spoon into an ungreased 2-quart casserole dish; set aside. Toss bread crumbs with margarine; sprinkle over ziti. Bake at 350 degrees until top is golden, about 20 to 30 minutes.

Mary Beth Updike, Ottawa, IL

Chicken Noodle Casserole

My mom created this recipe and it is a favorite of mine. Nothing turns a day around quicker than coming home to this dish!

Makes 4 servings

2 T. margarine
2 T. all-purpose flour
1 t. chicken bouillon granules
1 c. boiling water
10-3/4 oz. can cream of chicken
    soup
1-1/2 c. cooked chicken, diced
8-oz. pkg. wide egg noodles, cooked
1 c. potato chips, crushed

Melt margarine in a large saucepan over medium heat; stir in flour. Dissolve bouillon in boiling water; add to pan. Stir in soup and chicken; heat through. Add noodles; pour into a greased 2-quart casserole dish. Sprinkle with crushed chips. Bake, uncovered, at 325 degrees for 15 minutes.

Zippy Ziti & Broccoli

Annette Lavery, Belmont, MA

Baked Chicken Jambalaya

Looking for a flavorful new dinner recipe? The whole family will love this one!

Makes 8 servings

1 lb. smoked beef sausage, sliced
1/4 c. butter
4 c. cooked chicken, cubed
16-oz. pkg. frozen mixed vegetables, thawed
1 onion, sliced
4 stalks celery, sliced
1 green pepper, thinly sliced
2 c. shredded mozzarella or Cheddar cheese
16-oz. pkg. bowtie pasta, cooked

In a skillet over medium-high heat, sauté sausage in butter until browned. Add chicken to skillet with sausage; stir well. Transfer sausage mixture to an ungreased 13"x9" baking pan; add mixed vegetables, onion, celery and green pepper. Top with cheese; cover with aluminum foil. Bake at 350 degrees for about 30 minutes, until vegetables are crisp-tender and cheese is melted. To serve, ladle sausage mixture over cooked pasta.

★ TIME-SAVING SHORTCUT ★ Canned and frozen vegetables are flash-packed soon after being harvested, and they're convenient to keep on hand. If you have fresh-picked veggies available, by all means use them. Generally speaking, a 16-ounce can (drained) or a 16-ounce frozen package equals about 2 cups vegetables.

Baked Chicken Jambalaya

Karen Brown, Palm Springs, CA

Linguine with Garlic Sauce

If you like extra cheese, a sprinkle of grated Parmesan tops this pasta perfectly.

Makes 6 servings

6 T. butter
16-oz. pkg. sliced mushrooms
6 cloves garlic, minced
1 t. dried rosemary
1/2 t. pepper
1/2-pt. container whipping cream
8-oz. pkg. linguine pasta, cooked
8-oz. pkg. shredded mozzarella cheese
salt to taste
Garnish: chopped fresh parsley

Melt butter in a skillet over medium heat; add mushrooms, garlic and seasonings. Sauté for 5 minutes, until mushrooms release their juices, stirring occasionally. Stir in cream; simmer until thickened slightly, about 3 minutes. Add linguine, cheese and salt to taste; stir until cheese melts. Sprinkle with parsley.

Ashley Jones, Greenville, OH

Easy Chicken Fettuccine

Recently I tried this for the first time... it's delicious and ready in 20 minutes! People keep asking me for the recipe and I am happy to share.

Makes 6 servings

8-oz. pkg. cream cheese, cubed
3/4 c. grated Parmesan cheese
1/2 c. butter, sliced
1/2 c. milk
1 lb. boneless, skinless chicken breasts, cubed
1 T. oil
12-oz. pkg. fettuccine pasta, cooked

Combine cheeses, butter and milk in a saucepan. Stir continuously over medium heat until cheeses melt and mixture is smooth; keep warm. In a large, deep skillet over medium-high heat, cook chicken in oil until juices run clear; drain. Add cooked pasta to skillet and top with cheese sauce; toss to mix well.

Linguine with Garlic Sauce

Carrie O'Shea, Marina Del Rey, CA

Too-Much-Zucchini Stovetop Dinner

A scrumptious hearty dish for when your garden is overflowing with zucchini!

Serves 6 to 8

3 c. elbow macaroni, uncooked
2 T. olive oil
1 onion, chopped
2 cloves garlic, minced
1 lb. ground beef
1/2 lb. ground Italian pork sausage
3 to 4 zucchini, quartered and sliced 1/2-inch thick
14-1/2 oz. can crushed tomatoes
26-oz. jar spaghetti sauce
6-oz. can tomato paste
1/2 c. water
1/2 t. dried basil
1/2 t. dried oregano
1/2 t. garlic powder
salt and pepper to taste
8-oz. pkg. shredded mozzarella cheese

Cook macaroni according to package directions; drain. Meanwhile, add oil to a large cast-iron skillet over medium heat. Sauté onion and garlic until tender, about 5 minutes. Add beef and sausage; cook until browned. Drain; stir in zucchini, tomatoes with juice and remaining ingredients except salt, pepper and mozzarella cheese. Cover and simmer for 10 to 15 minutes, until zucchini is tender. Add seasonings; top with cheese. Serve zucchini mixture ladled over cooked macaroni.

★ KID-FRIENDLY ★ Just for fun, cut slices of crunchy carrot, zucchini and radish into stars, flowers and other fun shapes with mini cookie cutters...kids will eat their veggies happily!

Too-Much-Zucchini Stovetop Dinner

Barb Gilbert, Helena, MT

Ham & Cheese Spaghetti

Real comfort food...a great way to make something delicious with leftover ham.

Serves 4 to 6

1 lb. cooked ham, cubed
1 to 2 t. olive oil
1 green pepper, diced
1 onion, diced
2 to 3 cloves garlic, minced
15-oz. can tomato sauce
14-1/2 oz. can diced tomatoes
Italian seasoning to taste
16-oz. pkg. spaghetti, uncooked
16-oz. pkg. sliced American cheese

In a skillet over medium heat, lightly brown ham in oil. Add pepper and onion; sauté until tender. Stir in garlic, tomato sauce, tomatoes with juice and seasoning; bring to a boil. Reduce heat; cover and simmer for 20 to 30 minutes, stirring occasionally. Meanwhile, cook spaghetti according to package directions; drain. In a greased 13"x9" baking pan, place a layer of spaghetti, a layer of ham mixture and 3 to 4 cheese slices. Repeat layering 2 to 3 times, ending with sauce and cheese. Bake, uncovered, at 375 degrees for about 10 minutes, until hot and bubbly.

★ SPICY SECRET ★ If you use lots of Italian seasoning, mix up your own to store in a shaker jar...you may already have the ingredients in your spice rack. A good basic blend is 2 tablespoons each of dried oregano, basil, thyme, marjoram and rosemary. Add or subtract to suit your taste.

Ham & Cheese Spaghetti

Joellen Jubara, Uniontown, OH

Beef Chow Fun

This homemade version of a take-out classic is sure to tingle your taste buds. Look for wide rice noodles in the Asian section of your grocery store or at a Chinese market.

Makes 4 servings

1/2 c. sherry or beef broth
4 t. black bean-garlic sauce
1 T. soy sauce
2 t. light brown sugar, packed
2 t. cornstarch
4 t. oil, divided
1 t. fresh ginger, peeled and minced
12-oz. pkg. frozen stir-fry vegetables
1/2 c. water, divided
8-oz. pkg. wide rice noodles, cooked
8-oz. sirloin beef steak, thinly sliced

In a bowl, combine sherry or broth, sauces, brown sugar and cornstarch; set aside. Heat 2 teaspoons oil in a skillet over medium heat. Cook ginger for 30 seconds. Add vegetables and 1/4 cup water; cover and cook, stirring occasionally, until vegetables are tender, about 3 minutes. Combine vegetables and cooked noodles in a bowl; set aside. Heat remaining oil in the same skillet over medium-high heat. Add steak; cook and stir until browned. Stir in sauce mixture; cook until thickened. Return noodle mixture to pan with remaining 1/4 cup water. Cook and stir until evenly coated and warmed through.

★ HOT TIP ★ Like to top your dishes with sesame seeds? Toasting really brings out the flavor of sesame seeds and chopped nuts...and it's simple. Add seeds or nuts to a small dry skillet. Cook and stir over low heat for a few minutes, until toasty and golden.

Beef Chow Fun

PASTA BOWLS

Donna Nowicki, Center City, MN

Shrimp Monterey

Garlic and shrimp...what a scrumptious combination! Serve over buttered spinach fettuccine.

Serves 4 to 6

2 cloves garlic, minced
2 T. butter
2 lbs. uncooked medium shrimp, peeled and cleaned
1/2 c. white wine or chicken broth
2 c. shredded Monterey Jack cheese
2 T. fresh parsley, minced

In a skillet over medium heat, sauté garlic in butter for one minute. Add shrimp; cook for 4 to 5 minutes, or until pink. Using a slotted spoon, transfer shrimp to a greased 11"x7" baking pan; set aside and keep warm. Pour wine or broth into skillet; bring to a boil. Cook and stir for 5 minutes. Pour over shrimp; top with cheese and parsley. Bake, uncovered, at 350 degrees for 10 minutes, or until cheese is melted.

Bev Fisher, Mesa, AZ

Ranch Chicken & Noodles

Most people like chicken and will enjoy this recipe as much as I do. When I serve it to company, they always ask for the recipe.

Serves 4 to 6

6 slices bacon, cut into narrow strips
4 boneless, skinless chicken breasts, cut into bite-size pieces
2 T. all-purpose flour
2 T. ranch salad dressing mix
1-1/4 c. milk
8-oz. pkg. medium egg noodles, cooked
Garnish: grated Parmesan cheese

In a skillet over medium heat, cook bacon until crisp. Drain bacon on paper towels; reserve 2 tablespoons drippings in skillet. Cook chicken in reserved drippings until tender and golden on all sides. Sprinkle flour and dressing mix over chicken in skillet; stir in milk. Cook and stir until thickened and bubbly. Cook and stir for one minute more. Stir in bacon. Serve chicken and sauce over cooked noodles, sprinkled with cheese.

Shrimp Monterey

JoAnn, Gooseberry Patch

Inside-Out Ravioli

Just add a crisp tossed salad with oil & vinegar dressing for a hearty Italian-style meal. Please pass the Parmesan!

Makes 10 servings

16-oz. pkg. small shell or bowtie pasta, uncooked
1 lb. ground beef
1 c. onion, chopped
1/2 c. dry bread crumbs
1 egg, beaten
1 t. Italian seasoning
1 t. salt
1 t. pepper
8-oz. pkg. sliced mushrooms
10-oz. pkg. frozen chopped spinach, thawed and drained

16-oz. jar spaghetti sauce
1 c. shredded mozzarella cheese
Garnish: grated Parmesan cheese

Cook pasta according to package directions; drain. Meanwhile, brown beef with onion in a skillet over medium heat; drain. In a greased 13"x9" baking pan, combine cooked pasta, beef mixture and remaining ingredients except sauce and cheeses. Stir gently; top with sauce and mozzarella cheese. Bake, uncovered, at 350 degrees for 45 minutes, or until hot and bubbly. Sprinkle with Parmesan cheese at serving time.

★ SAVVY SIDE ★ Serving an Italian meal tonight? Whip up some warm garlic bread...it can't be beat! Mix 1/2 cup melted butter and 2 teaspoons minced garlic; spread over a split loaf of Italian bread. Sprinkle with chopped fresh parsley. Bake at 350 degrees for 8 minutes, or until hot, then broil briefly, until golden. Cut into generous slices.

Inside-Out Ravioli

Dawn Dhooghe, Concord, NC

Scallops & Shrimp with Linguine

Everyone will love this!

Makes 8 servings

3 T. butter, divided
3 T. olive oil, divided
1 lb. uncooked large shrimp, peeled and cleaned
3 cloves garlic, minced and divided
1 lb. uncooked sea scallops
8-oz. pkg. sliced mushrooms
2 c. snow peas, trimmed
2 tomatoes, chopped
1/2 c. green onions, chopped
1 t. salt
1/2 t. red pepper flakes
1/4 c. fresh parsley, chopped
2 T. fresh basil, chopped
10-oz. pkg. linguine pasta, cooked and kept warm
Garnish: grated Parmesan cheese

Heat one tablespoon each of butter and olive oil in a large skillet over medium-high heat. Add shrimp and half of garlic; cook 2 to 3 minutes, until shrimp turn pink. Remove shrimp from skillet; keep warm. Repeat with scallops, one tablespoon butter, one tablespoon oil and remaining garlic. Heat remaining one tablespoon each of butter and oil in same skillet over medium heat. Add mushrooms, snow peas, tomatoes, green onions, salt, pepper flakes, parsley and basil; cook 4 to 5 minutes. Combine linguine, mushroom mixture, shrimp and scallops in a large bowl; toss well. Sprinkle with Parmesan cheese.

Scallops & Shrimp with Linguine

Hearty Meatball Stew, Page 196

CHAPTER FIVE

Slow-Cooker Meals in a Bowl

Chicken Pot Pie Stew, Page 216

Cashew Chicken, Page 206

Lynda Robson, Boston, MA

Overnight Cherry Oatmeal

Assemble the night before and wake to the aroma of cherry pie...what a great way to start the day!

Serves 4 to 6

3 c. long-cooking oats, uncooked
3/4 c. powdered sugar
1/4 t. salt
21-oz. can cherry pie filling
6 c. water
1 t. almond extract

Combine oats, powdered sugar and salt in a large bowl; pour into a slow cooker that has been sprayed with non-stick vegetable spray. Add remaining ingredients; stir until combined. Cover and cook on low setting for 8 hours.

Laurie Wilson, Fort Wayne, IN

Laurie's Cozy Oatmeal

There's nothing like a bowl of this warming oatmeal with a dash of milk or cream on a chilly fall morning.

Makes 4 servings

2 c. milk
1 c. long-cooking oats, uncooked
1 c. Granny Smith apple, peeled, cored and chopped
1/2 c. raisins
1/2 c. chopped pecans
1/4 c. brown sugar, packed
1 T. butter, melted
2 T. maple syrup
1 t. cinnamon

Place all ingredients in a lightly greased slow cooker; mix well. Cover and cook on low setting for 7 to 8 hours. Stir before serving.

★ TIME-SAVING SHORTCUT ★ **Early risers will appreciate a crockery cooker of Overnight Cherry Oatmeal! Set out brown sugar and a small bottle of cream on ice so everyone can top their own.**

Overnight Cherry Oatmeal

Emily Martin, Ontario, Canada

Sleep-Over Breakfast Strata

Every year at Christmas, we're sure to have some of my relatives staying for the holidays. This recipe fills up our hungry crowd, and everyone loves it.

Serves 8 to 10

4 c. day-old white bread, cubed
8 eggs
1-1/2 c. milk
1/2 t. salt
1/2 t. pepper
8-oz. pkg. shredded Cheddar cheese
8-oz. pkg. sliced mushrooms
3/4 lb. bacon, crisply cooked and
   crumbled

Place bread in a 6-quart slow cooker sprayed with a non-stick vegetable spray; set aside. Beat eggs in a large bowl. Whisk in milk, salt and pepper; stir in cheese and mushrooms. Pour egg mixture evenly over bread; set aside. Cook bacon in a skillet over medium heat until crisp; drain, crumble and sprinkle over top. Cover and cook on low setting for 6 to 8 hours, until eggs have set and top is lightly golden. Uncover and let stand for several minutes before serving.

Amy Butcher, Columbus, GA

That's a Gouda Breakfast!

There's something about the salty taste of Gouda cheese with the savory tartness of the sun-dried tomatoes that makes this slow-cooker breakfast one I return to again & again.

Makes 6 servings

5 baking potatoes, peeled, cooked and
   shredded
18 links pork breakfast sausage, sliced
2 c. shredded Gouda cheese
1/2 c. sun-dried tomatoes packed in oil,
   drained and thinly sliced
1/3 c. onion, finely chopped
1 doz. eggs
1/2 c. milk
salt and pepper to taste
Garnish: salsa

Place half the potatoes in the bottom of a lightly greased slow cooker. Sprinkle with half the sausage, one cup cheese and all the sun-dried tomatoes and onion. Top with remaining potatoes and sausage. In a bowl, beat together eggs, milk, salt and pepper; pour over potato mixture. Top with remaining cheese. Cover and cook on low setting for 6 to 7 hours, until eggs are set. Top servings with salsa.

Sleep-Over Breakfast Strata

Megan Brooks, Antioch, TN

Ham & Lentil Soup

A warm and comforting meal at the end of the day!

Makes 6 servings

3 c. chicken broth
3 c. water
1 c. cooked ham, diced
1-1/2 c. celery, chopped
1-1/2 c. baby carrots, thinly sliced
1 onion, thinly sliced
1 c. dried lentils
1-1/2 t. dried thyme
3 c. fresh baby spinach
Garnish: shredded Parmesan cheese

In a 5-quart slow cooker, combine all ingredients except spinach and garnish. Stir well. Cover and cook on low setting for 7 to 8 hours. Stir in spinach; let stand for a few minutes, until wilted. Garnish each serving with a sprinkle of cheese.

★ TIME-SAVING SHORTCUT ★
A time-saving tip...slice & dice meats and veggies the night before, place in separate plastic zipping bags and pop in the fridge. In the morning, toss everything into the slow cooker and you're on your way.

Marie Matter, Dallas, TX

Vegetarian Quinoa Chili

This hearty chili couldn't be easier.

Makes 6 servings

2 14-1/2 oz. cans diced tomatoes
    with green chiles
15-oz. can tomato sauce
15-oz. can kidney beans, drained
    and rinsed
15-oz. can black beans, drained
    and rinsed
1-1/2 c. vegetable broth
1 c. frozen corn
1 c. quinoa, uncooked and rinsed
1 onion, diced
3 cloves garlic, minced
2 T. chili powder
2 t. ground cumin
1-1/2 t. smoked paprika
1-1/2 t. sugar
1/4 t. cayenne pepper
1/2 t. ground coriander
1/2 t. kosher salt
1/4 t. pepper
Garnish: shredded Cheddar cheese,
    sour cream, sliced avocado, chopped
    fresh cilantro

Combine undrained tomatoes and remaining ingredients except garnish in a slow cooker; stir together. Cover and cook on low setting for 6 to 8 hours, or on high setting for 3 to 4 hours. To serve, ladle into soup bowls; garnish as desired.

Ham & Lentil Soup

Amy Bradsher, Roxboro, NC

Caribbean Chicken & Veggies

I love to serve meals made from scratch, but they can be pretty time-consuming. This recipe is super-simple and cooks on its own, requiring little attention from me. Best of all, my kids love it!

Serves 4 to 6

1 lb. boneless, skinless chicken tenders
1 c. canned diced pineapple with juice
1 onion, coarsely chopped
1 green pepper, coarsely chopped
3/4 c. Caribbean-style marinade
2 c. canned black beans, drained
1 lb. broccoli, cut into bite-size flowerets
cooked rice

Combine chicken, pineapple with juice, onion, green pepper and marinade in a slow cooker. Cover and cook on low setting for 4 to 5 hours, until chicken is nearly cooked. Add black beans and broccoli. Cover and cook for another hour, or until broccoli is tender. Serve chicken mixture over cooked rice.

Tina Knotts, Cable, OH

Western Omelet Crockery Casserole

Let your slow cooker do all the work overnight. The next morning, you'll have a hot, filling breakfast ready to enjoy!

Serves 6 to 8

32-oz. pkg. frozen shredded hashbrowns
1 lb. bacon, crisply cooked and crumbled
1 onion, diced
1 green pepper, diced
1-1/2 c. shredded Cheddar or Monterey Jack cheese
1 doz. eggs
1 c. milk
1 t. salt
1 t. pepper
Optional: hot pepper sauce

In a greased slow cooker, layer frozen hashbrowns, bacon, onion, green pepper and cheese. Repeat layering 2 to 3 more times, ending with cheese; set aside. Whisk together eggs, milk, salt and pepper; pour over ingredients in slow cooker. Cover and cook on low setting for 10 to 12 hours. Serve with hot sauce, if desired.

Caribbean Chicken & Veggies

Lisa Sett, Thousand Oaks, CA

Slow-Cooker Chile Verde Soup

Hearty, filling and goes together in a hurry!

Serves 6 to 8

1/2 lb. pork tenderloin, cut into
   1/2-inch cubes
1 t. oil
2 c. chicken broth
2 15-oz. cans white beans, drained
   and rinsed
2 4-oz. cans diced green chiles
1/4 t. ground cumin
1/4 t. dried oregano
salt and pepper to taste
Optional: chopped fresh cilantro

Cook pork in oil in a skillet over medium heat for one to 2 minutes or until browned. Place pork in a 4-quart slow cooker. Add remaining ingredients except cilantro; stir well. Cover and cook on low setting for 4 to 6 hours. Sprinkle cilantro over each serving, if desired.

Cathy Hillier, Salt Lake City, UT

Chicken Stroganoff

This easy recipe is delectable served over egg noodles. My family doesn't care for mushrooms, but if yours does, be sure to add some.

Makes 4 servings

4 boneless, skinless chicken breasts,
   cubed
2 T. margarine, diced
0.7-oz. pkg. Italian salad dressing mix
10-3/4 oz. can cream of chicken soup
8-oz. pkg. cream cheese, cubed

Place chicken, margarine and dressing mix in a slow cooker; toss to mix well. Cover and cook on low setting for 5 to 6 hours. Stir in soup and cream cheese. Cover; turn setting to high and cook for 30 minutes, until heated through.

★ HOT TIP ★ A covered slow cooker cooks with little or no evaporation...all the delicious cooking juices combine to create a scrumptious gravy. Just add the amount of liquid that the recipe calls for.

Slow-Cooker Chile Verde Soup

Karen Swartz, Woodville, OH

Hearty Meatball Stew

Busy day ahead? Prepare the ingredients for this easy recipe the night before. For a special treat, serve it ladled into individual sourdough bread bowls.

Makes 8 servings

1 lb. new potatoes, cubed
16-oz. pkg. baby carrots
1 onion, sliced
2 4-oz. cans sliced mushrooms, drained
16-oz. pkg. frozen meatballs
12-oz. jar beef gravy
14-1/2 oz. can Italian seasoned diced tomatoes
3-1/4 c. water
pepper to taste
14-1/2 oz. can corn, drained

In a large slow cooker, layer all ingredients except corn in the order listed. Cover and cook on low setting for 8 to 10 hours. About one hour before serving, stir in corn.

Pamela Stump, Chino Hills, CA

Turkey & Spinach Lasagna

Whenever I used no-boil lasagna noodles in casseroles, I never felt that they were cooked thoroughly. So I tried them in my slow cooker, thinking that it would be more moist... it worked!

Serves 6 to 8

1 lb. ground turkey
1 t. dried oregano
salt and pepper to taste
15-oz. container ricotta cheese
8-oz. pkg. shredded mozzarella cheese
10-oz. pkg. frozen spinach, cooked and drained
9-oz. pkg. no-boil lasagna noodles, uncooked and broken to fit
26-oz. jar spaghetti sauce with mushrooms
1/4 c. hot water

In a skillet over medium heat, brown turkey with seasonings; drain. Mix together cheeses and spinach. Layer as follows in a slow cooker: half of dry noodles, half of turkey, half of sauce and half of cheese mixture. Repeat layers in same order, ending with cheese. Pour hot water over all. Cover and cook on low setting for 4-1/2 hours. Let stand for a few minutes before serving.

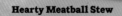
Hearty Meatball Stew

Joanne Curran, Arlington, MA

Slow-Cooker Country Chicken & Dumplings

Add some sliced carrots or peas to sneak in a few veggies if you like!

Makes 6 servings

4 boneless, skinless chicken breasts
2 10-3/4 oz. cans cream of chicken
   soup
2 T. butter, sliced
1 onion, finely diced
2 7-1/2 oz. tubes refrigerated
   biscuits, torn

Place chicken, soup, butter and onion in a 4-quart slow cooker; add enough water to cover chicken. Cover and cook on high setting for 4 hours. Add biscuits to slow cooker; gently push biscuits into cooking liquid. Cover and continue cooking for about 1-1/2 hours, until biscuits are done in the center.

Kerry Mayer, Dunham Springs, LA

Creole Beef & Noodles

This dish tastes like it took a lot of effort, but stirs up in a jiffy! The night before, I move the beef from the freezer into the fridge. In the morning, it slices easily while still partly frozen.

Serves 3 to 4

3/4 lb. beef round steak, sliced into
   thin strips
1 green pepper, chopped
1 onion, chopped
1 tomato, chopped
1 clove garlic, pressed
1 t. dried parsley
1/2 t. salt
1/8 t. pepper
1 cube beef bouillon
1/2 c. boiling water
2 T. cornstarch
2 T. cold water
cooked wide egg noodles

Combine beef, vegetables, garlic and seasonings in a slow cooker. Dissolve bouillon cube in boiling water; add to slow cooker. Cover and cook on low setting for 7 to 8 hours, until beef is tender. Shortly before serving time, dissolve cornstarch in cold water; stir into slow cooker. Turn to high setting. Cover and cook for about 10 minutes, until slightly thickened. To serve, spoon beef mixture over cooked noodles.

Slow-Cooker Country Chicken & Dumplings

Ronda Hauss, Louisville, KY

Spicy Bean & Turkey Sausage Stew

I use whatever beans I have on hand, but love a mix of colors and flavors. Use your favorites!

Makes 6 servings

1 lb. smoked turkey sausage, halved lengthwise and sliced
16-oz. can kidney beans, drained and rinsed
15-oz. can Great Northern beans, drained and rinsed
15-oz. can black beans, drained and rinsed
1 onion, chopped
3 cloves garlic, minced
1 red pepper, chopped
1-1/2 c. frozen corn
16-oz. jar salsa
1 c. water
1 t. ground cumin
1/2 t. pepper
hot pepper sauce to taste

In a 5-quart slow cooker, combine all ingredients. Cover and cook on low setting for 6 to 8 hours. Stir before serving.

Marcia Bills, Orleans, NE

Hearty Lasagna Soup

My daughters request this soup whenever they are coming home from college for weekends or holidays...in fact, our family calls it Coming Home Soup! It's so warm and delicious...we all love it.

Makes 6 servings

1 lb. ground beef, browned and drained
6.4-oz. pkg. ground beef lasagna dinner, divided
6 c. water
1 c. corn
15-oz. can Italian-style stewed tomatoes

Place beef in a slow cooker. Add lasagna sauce mix, water, corn and undrained tomatoes; stir well. Cover and cook on low setting for 4 to 6 hours. Mix in lasagna noodles and cook an additional 20 minutes, until noodles are tender.

Spicy Bean & Turkey Sausage Stew

Mignonne Gardner, Pleasant Grove, UT

Slow-Cooker Steak Chili

All summer I long for cool, crisp autumn nights. I created this recipe just for those fabulous fall nights. The aroma of chili fills my home while it simmers. It makes me giddy for Halloween!

Makes 8 servings

2 lbs. beef round steak, cut into
  1-inch cubes
1-1/2 c. onion, chopped
2 cloves garlic, minced
2 T. oil
1-1/3 c. water, divided
2 15-oz. cans kidney beans, drained
  and rinsed
2 14-1/2 oz. cans diced tomatoes
16-oz. jar salsa
15-oz. can tomato sauce
1 c. celery, chopped
1-1/2 T. chili powder
1 t. ground cumin
1 t. dried oregano
1/2 t. pepper
2 T. all-purpose flour
2 T. cornmeal
Garnish: shredded Cheddar cheese,
  sour cream, crushed tortilla chips

Brown beef, onion and garlic in oil in a large skillet over medium heat; drain. Add beef mixture to a 5-quart slow cooker. Stir in one cup water and remaining ingredients except flour, cornmeal and garnish; mix well. Cover and cook on low setting for 8 hours. Combine flour, cornmeal and remaining 1/3 cup water in a small bowl, whisking until smooth. Add mixture to simmering chili right before serving; stir 2 minutes, or until thickened. Garnish as desired.

★ SAVVY SIDE ★ Cornbread loves chili! If you like sweet cornbread, you'll love this family-size recipe. Mix together an 8-1/2 ounce box of corn muffin mix, a 9-ounce box of yellow cake mix, 1/2 cup water, 1/3 cup milk and 2 beaten eggs. Pour into a greased 13"x9" baking pan and bake at 350 degrees for 15 to 20 minutes. Scrumptious!

Slow-Cooker Steak Chili

Mary Little, Franklin, TN

Easy Chicken Chili

Our family loves to enjoy this dish on a chilly Tennessee evening.

Serves 8 to 10

2 to 3 5-oz. cans chicken
3 15-oz. cans Great Northern beans
2 15-1/2 oz. cans hominy
16-oz. jar salsa
2 8-oz. pkgs. shredded Monterey Jack cheese

Combine all ingredients in a slow cooker, including liquid from cans. Cover and cook on low setting for 8 hours.

★ SPICY SECRET ★ **If you love super-spicy chili, give New Mexico chili powder a try. It contains pure ground red chili peppers, unlike regular chili powder which is a blend of chili, garlic and other seasonings.**

JoAnn, Gooseberry Patch

Chicken Sausage & Pasta

While on vacation, we tried this dish at an Italian restaurant and loved it. I was really pleased with how well it turned out in a slow cooker...now we can enjoy it often!

Makes 4 servings

1/2 c. yellow onion, minced
1 clove garlic, minced
1 T. olive oil
1 lb. sweet Italian chicken sausage links, removed from casings and chopped
28-oz. can stewed tomatoes, drained
1-1/2 c. red or yellow pepper, sliced
3/4 c. fresh basil, chopped
red pepper flakes, salt and pepper to taste
cooked rotini pasta

In a skillet over medium heat, cook onion and garlic in oil until translucent. Add sausage to skillet; cook for several minutes, just until beginning to brown. Drain; transfer skillet mixture to a slow cooker. Add remaining ingredients except pasta; stir to blend. Cover and cook on high setting for 2-1/2 to 3 hours, until peppers are tender. Serve over cooked pasta.

Easy Chicken Chili

Anne Alesauskas, Minocqua, WI

Cashew Chicken

This is one of the simplest recipes in my recipe box and I think you'll love it! We just love Chinese food... unfortunately, our options aren't great for take-out, so I make my own whenever possible. Using the slow cooker is an added bonus on those days when you're running like mad.

Makes 4 servings

1/2 c. all-purpose flour
1/8 t. pepper
2 lbs. boneless, skinless chicken
    breasts, cubed
2 T. canola oil
1/4 c. soy sauce
2 T. rice wine vinegar
2 T. catsup
1 T. brown sugar, packed
1 clove garlic, minced
1/2 t. fresh ginger, peeled and grated
red pepper flakes to taste
cooked brown rice
Garnish: 1/2 c. cashews

Combine flour and pepper in a plastic zipping bag. Add chicken pieces to bag; toss to coat and set aside. Heat oil in a large skillet over medium-high heat. Cook chicken for about 5 minutes, until golden on all sides but not cooked through. Transfer chicken to a slow cooker; set aside. In a small bowl, combine remaining ingredients except rice and cashews. Pour mixture over chicken, stirring slightly. Cover and cook on low setting for 3 to 4 hours, or on high setting for one to 2 hours, until chicken juices run clear. To serve, spoon chicken mixture over cooked rice; top with cashews.

★ FREEZE IT ★ Nuts, shelled or unshelled, will stay fresher longer if they're stored in the freezer. As an added benefit, unshelled nuts will crack much easier when frozen.

Cashew Chicken

Heather Garthus, Newfolden, MN

Cajun Crockery Breakfast

This makes a great breakfast-for-dinner supper. Add a dollop of sour cream to each serving...delicious!

Makes 10 servings

32-oz. pkg. frozen diced potatoes
2 c. ground pork breakfast sausage,
    browned
1 c. onion, finely chopped
1/2 c. green pepper, chopped
1/2 c. mushrooms, chopped
3 c. shredded sharp Cheddar cheese
1 doz. eggs
salt, pepper and Cajun seasoning
    to taste
1/4 c. milk

Place half the diced potatoes in a slow cooker; top with all of the sausage and half each of the onion, green pepper, mushrooms and cheese. Repeat layering once more, ending with cheese. In a bowl, beat together eggs, seasonings and milk. Pour egg mixture over ingredients in slow cooker. Cover and cook on high setting for 4 to 6 hours, until a toothpick inserted near the center tests clean.

Valerie Sholes, Minneapolis, MN

Bacon & Cheese Breakfast Casserole

This casserole is full of lots of tasty breakfast favorites...sure to please even the pickiest of eaters.

Serves 8 to 10

1 T. oil
1 onion, chopped
32-oz. pkg. frozen shredded
    hashbrowns, thawed
1 green pepper, chopped
1/2 lb. bacon, crisply cooked and
    crumbled
8-oz. pkg. shredded Cheddar cheese
8-oz. pkg. shredded mozzarella
    cheese
1 doz. eggs
1 c. skim milk
1 T. dried parsley
1 t. dry mustard
2 t. salt
1 t. pepper
Optional: additional shredded
    Cheddar cheese

Heat oil in a skillet over medium heat. Sauté onion in oil until translucent. Stir in hashbrowns and cook until golden. Place half the hashbrown mixture in a lightly greased slow cooker. Top hashbrown mixture with green pepper, bacon and cheeses; set aside. In a bowl, beat together eggs, milk, parsley, mustard, salt and pepper. Pour egg mixture over cheese in slow cooker. Cover and cook on low setting for 5 to 6 hours, until a knife tip tests clean. Sprinkle a little extra cheese on servings, if desired.

Cajun Crockery Breakfast

Michelle Collins, San Diego, CA

Collins' Best Lentil & Sausage Soup

A very good friend of mine who passed away used to make a lentil sausage soup that I adored, so whenever I make this, I think of him.

Serves 6 to 8

1 lb. Kielbasa turkey sausage, cut into 1/2-inch pieces
1 c. onion, chopped
1 c. celery, chopped
1 c. carrots, peeled and chopped
1 c. redskin potatoes, diced
2 T. fresh flat-leaf parsley, chopped
1/2 t. pepper
1/8 t. ground nutmeg
6 c. beef broth
1 c. dried lentils, rinsed and drained

Combine all ingredients except broth and lentils in a freezer-safe container. Refrigerate overnight, or freeze until ready to use.

To cook:

Thaw sausage mixture overnight in refrigerator if frozen. Combine soup mixture with broth and dried lentils in a slow cooker. Cover and cook on low setting for 6 to 8 hours; stir before serving.

★ TIME-SAVING SHORTCUT ★ This make-ahead soup is so handy to have ready for a busy day. These ingredients don't have to be refrigerated overnight though. Just add everything to your slow cooker and follow the cooking instructions for delicious, same-day soup!

Collins' Best Lentil & Sausage Soup

Ramona Storm, Gardner, IL

Easy Chicken & Noodles

This smells so good and warms you up on a cold day. Leftover cooked chicken works great. Add some warm, crusty bread and a citrus salad...dinner is served!

Makes 8 servings

16-oz. pkg. frozen egg noodles, uncooked
2 14-1/2 oz. cans chicken broth
2 10-3/4 oz. cans cream of chicken soup
1/2 c. onion, finely chopped
1/2 c. carrot, peeled and diced
1/2 c. celery, diced
salt and pepper to taste
2 c. boneless, skinless chicken breasts, cooked and cubed

Thaw egg noodles (or run package under warm water) just enough to break apart; set aside. Spray a slow cooker with non-stick vegetable spray. Add remaining ingredients except chicken; blend well. Stir in noodles and chicken. Cover and cook on low setting for 7 to 8 hours, until hot and bubbly.

Ronda Hauss, Louisville, KY

Firehouse Chicken

My stepfather, a former firefighter, taught me how to make this easy, delicious dish. It was a hit at the firehouse, too! The sauce is also wonderful over fresh-baked bread.

Makes 4 servings

2 10-3/4 oz. cans cream of mushroom soup
14-1/2 oz. can chicken broth
6-oz. jar sliced mushrooms, drained
1.35-oz. pkg. onion soup mix
2 lbs. boneless, skinless chicken breasts, cubed if desired
cooked rice

Mix all ingredients except chicken and rice in a slow cooker until well combined. Add chicken; stir to coat. Cover and cook on low setting for 8 hours, or for 4 hours on high setting. To serve, spoon over cooked rice.

★ HOT TIP ★ Perfectly cooked rice...as easy as 1-2-3! One cup long-cooking rice plus 2 cups water equals 3 cups cooked rice. Stir rice into boiling water, cover and simmer over low heat for 20 minutes. Leave the pan lid on for a few minutes more, then fluff with a fork.

Easy Chicken & Noodles

Lisa Hays, Crocker, MO

Garden-Style Fettuccine

The perfect dinner to make good use of all those veggies from your garden.

Serves 6 to 8

1 zucchini, sliced 1/4 inch thick
1 yellow squash, sliced 1/4 inch thick
2 carrots, peeled and thinly sliced
1-1/2 c. sliced mushrooms
10-oz. pkg. frozen broccoli cuts
4 green onions, sliced
1 clove garlic, minced
1/2 t. dried basil
1/4 t. salt
1/2 t. pepper
1 c. grated Parmesan cheese
12-oz. pkg. fettuccine pasta, cooked
1 c. shredded mozzarella cheese
1 c. milk
2 egg yolks, beaten

Place vegetables, seasonings and Parmesan cheese in a slow cooker. Cover and cook on high setting for 2 hours. Add remaining ingredients to slow cooker, stir well. Reduce heat to low setting; cover and cook an additional 14 to 30 minutes.

Kerry Mayer, Dunham Springs, LA

Creole Shrimp & Sausage

We used to live on the Gulf, and I would watch the shrimping boats come in and go out all the time. I'd be sure to pick up some fresh shrimp to make this delectable dish too!

Makes 6 servings

1 onion, chopped
1 green pepper, chopped
2 stalks celery, sliced
2 carrots, peeled and diced
4 cloves garlic, minced
14-1/2 oz. can diced tomatoes
3/4 c. chicken broth
2 t. Creole seasoning
3 andouille pork sausage links, cut into 1/2-inch pieces
10-oz. pkg. frozen corn, thawed
1 T. tomato paste
1 lb. large shrimp, peeled and cleaned
cooked rice

In a large bowl, combine onion, pepper, celery, carrots, garlic, tomatoes with juice, broth and seasoning. Mix well; stir in sausage and corn. Add mixture to a lightly greased slow cooker. Cover and cook on low setting for 8 hours. Stir in tomato paste and shrimp. Cover and cook for 7 to 10 more minutes, until shrimp is cooked. Spoon over rice to serve.

Garden-Style Fettuccine

Joyceann Dreibelbis, Wooster, OH

Chicken Pot Pie Stew

This comfort food will remind you of chicken pot pie...but there's no need to make a crust. I like to bake crescent roll dough flat on a baking sheet to form toppers.

Serves 12 to 15

4 boneless, skinless chicken thighs
    or breasts, cubed
10-3/4 oz. can cream of chicken soup
1 c. chicken broth
5 redskin potatoes, cubed
1 c. carrots, peeled and chopped
1 c. celery, chopped
1/4 c. onion, chopped
1 t. garlic, minced
1 t. celery seed
1 t. pepper
16-oz. pkg. frozen mixed vegetables
Optional: refrigerated crescent rolls
    or biscuits, baked

In a large slow cooker, combine all ingredients except frozen vegetables and rolls or biscuits. Cover and cook on low setting for 4 to 5 hours. Stir in frozen vegetables; cover and cook on low setting for one additional hour. If desired, top servings with baked crescent rolls or split biscuits.

Zoe Bennett, Columbia, SC

Slow-Cooker Corned Beef Hash

Top each serving with an egg cooked sunny-side up for a real stick-to-your-ribs breakfast.

Makes 8 servings

1 onion, chopped
3 stalks celery, chopped
3 cloves garlic, chopped
1 T. oil
1 T. Worcestershire sauce
1/4 t. Italian seasoning
salt and pepper to taste
12-oz. can corned beef, chopped
3 to 4 potatoes, peeled and cubed
2 10-1/2 oz. cans chicken broth

In a skillet over medium heat, sauté onion, celery and garlic in oil until tender. Stir in sauce and seasonings; combine with remaining ingredients in a slow cooker. Cover and cook on low setting for 5 to 6 hours.

Chicken Pot Pie Stew

Alison Carbonara, Grove City, OH

Slow-Cooker Steak & Red Pepper Bowls

Add a good shake of red pepper flakes right before serving for a little extra kick!

Makes 4 servings

2-1/2 lbs. beef chuck roast, thinly
    sliced and fat trimmed
1 t. salt, divided
1 t. pepper, divided
2 T. olive oil
1 c. beef broth
3 T. soy sauce
2 T. tomato paste
3 red peppers, sliced
1 yellow onion, sliced
5-oz. pkg. yellow rice, uncooked
Garnish: fresh cilantro, sour cream

Sprinkle beef with 1/2 teaspoon each salt and pepper. Heat oil in a skillet over medium-high heat. Working in batches, brown beef on both sides, about one minute per side; set aside. In a bowl, whisk together broth, soy sauce and tomato paste. Layer peppers and onion in a 5-quart slow cooker; sprinkle with remaining salt and pepper. Place beef on top of vegetables; pour broth mixture over all. Cover and cook on low setting for 6 to 7 hours, until beef is tender. About 30 minutes before serving, cook rice according to package directions. To serve, divide rice among 4 bowls; top with beef and vegetables. Garnish with cilantro and sour cream.

★ SAVVY SECRET ★ To get richer-tasting tomato paste, pick up sun-dried tomato paste in a tube.

Slow-Cooker Steak & Red Pepper Bowls

Vickie, Gooseberry Patch

Slow-Cooker Chicken Burrito Bowls with Corn Salsa

Fresh sweet corn tastes best for this salsa, but i've made it with frozen and even canned corn with good results.

Makes 4 servings

1 lb. boneless, skinless chicken breasts
1/2 t. chipotle chili powder
1 c. favorite salsa
2 t. olive oil
1 c. brown rice, uncooked
2 c. chicken broth or water
2 T. lime juice, divided
15-1/2 oz. can black beans, drained and rinsed
Garnish: 1/2 c. shredded Cheddar cheese, salsa, avocado slices, sour cream

Place chicken in a 4-quart slow cooker; sprinkle with chili powder. Spoon salsa over chicken. Cover and cook on low setting for 6 to 7 hours, or on high setting for 3 to 4 hours, until chicken is very tender. Shred chicken in slow cooker with 2 forks; keep slow cooker on low setting until ready to serve. About one hour before serving, add oil and rice to a saucepan over medium heat. Toast rice in oil for 3 to 5 minutes, stirring often. Add broth or water; bring mixture to a boil. Reduce heat to low; cover and simmer for 45 minutes. Remove from heat. Stir in lime juice; cover and let stand for 10 minutes. To serve, divide rice, chicken, black beans and Corn Salsa among 4 bowls. Garnish as desired.

Corn Salsa:

1 c. corn
1/2 c. red onion, diced
1/4 c. fresh cilantro, chopped
2 T. lime juice
salt and pepper to taste

Combine corn, onion, cilantro and lime juice in a bowl. Season with salt and pepper.

★ HOT TIP ★ Using fresh sweet corn in a recipe? When boiling corn, add sugar to the water instead of salt. Sugar will sweeten the corn while salt will make it tough.

Slow-Cooker Chicken Burrito Bowls with Corn Salsa

Rogene Rogers, Bemidji, MN

Pork Chops
à la Orange

We love these flavors together!

Serves 6 to 8

3 lbs. pork chops
salt and pepper to taste
2 c. orange juice
2 11-oz. cans mandarin oranges,
   drained
8-oz. can pineapple tidbits,
   drained
cooked egg noodles

Sprinkle pork chops with salt and pepper; place in a slow cooker. Pour orange juice over pork. Cover and cook on low setting for 6 to 8 hours, or on high setting for 3 to 4 hours. About 30 minutes before serving, add oranges and pineapple; continue cooking just until warm. Serve with cooked noodles.

Peggy Donnally, Toledo, OH

Sunday Beef
& Noodles

Noodles and potatoes...that's my idea of heaven on a plate!

Serves 6 to 8

2-lb. beef chuck roast
4 c. beef broth
1 c. onion, chopped
2 t. onion powder
1 t. garlic powder
1 T. dried parsley
salt and pepper to taste
16-oz. pkg. extra wide egg noodles,
   cooked
mashed potatoes

Place roast in a slow cooker. Combine broth, onion and seasonings; pour over roast. Cover and cook on low setting for 6 to 8 hours. Remove roast; slice and return to slow cooker. Add noodles to slow cooker; heat through. Serve over mashed potatoes.

★ TIME-SAVING SHORTCUT ★ A side dish time-saver. Purchase packaged mashed potatoes at the grocery store. Heat up, blend in sour cream and cream cheese to taste, then heat up again until well blended...so yummy!

Pork Chops à la Orange

First-Prize Peach Cobbler, Page 234

CHAPTER SIX

Desserts in a Bowl

Pineapple-Cherry Crisp, Page 242

Cookies & Cream Dessert, Page 246

Julie Hutson, Callahan, FL

Julie's Strawberry Yum-Yum

A wonderful, lighter strawberry trifle that's a snap to put together...this recipe is a winner!

Serves 8 to 10

2 3.3-oz. pkgs. instant sugar-free
   white chocolate pudding mix
4 c. 1% milk
1 baked angel food cake, torn into
   bite-size pieces and divided
2 to 4 c. fresh strawberries, hulled,
   sliced and divided
2 8-oz. containers fat-free frozen
   whipped topping, thawed
10-oz. pkg. coconut macaroon
   cookies, crushed and divided

Beat dry pudding mix and milk with an electric mixer on low speed for 2 minutes. Chill for a few minutes, until thickened. In a large trifle bowl, layer half each of cake pieces, pudding and strawberries, one container whipped topping and half of crushed cookies. Repeat layers, ending with cookies. Cover and chill until serving time.

Sandra Sullivan, Aurora, CO

Cranberry Bread Pudding

This is the ultimate comfort food. It's a favorite fall recipe for when time is short and the oven is full. You can substitute half-and-half for the whole milk or add chopped dried apples or other dried fruits for a tasty twist.

Makes 8 servings

4 c. whole milk
4 eggs
1 c. sugar
2 t. vanilla extract
1/2 t. salt
Optional: 2 T. brandy
6 c. white bread cubes, toasted
1-1/2 c. sweetened dried cranberries
Garnish: powdered sugar, whipped
   topping

In a bowl, beat milk, eggs, sugar, vanilla, salt and brandy, if using. Place bread cubes and cranberries in a large slow cooker; drizzle egg mixture over bread mixture. Stir to coat evenly. Cover and cook on low setting for about 3-1/2 hours, just until pudding is set. Sprinkle servings with powdered sugar and top with a dollop of whipped topping.

Julie's Strawberry Yum-Yum

Edith Beck, Elk Grove, CA

Wild Blackberry Cobbler

A very old recipe that a friend shared with me in high school. Every year, we pick wild blackberries together so I can make this cobbler.

Serves 4 to 6

1/2 c. butter, sliced
3 c. fresh blackberries
1/4 c. plus 2 T. water, divided
1-1/4 c. sugar, divided
1/2 t. cinnamon
2 T. cornstarch
1 c. all-purpose flour
1-1/2 t. baking powder
1/4 t. salt
1 c. milk

Add butter to a 9"x9" baking pan. Place in oven at 400 degrees until melted. Meanwhile, in a small saucepan, combine blackberries, 1/4 cup water, 1/4 cup sugar and cinnamon. Simmer over medium heat, stirring gently. Stir together cornstarch and remaining water until pourable; stir into berry mixture and cook until thickened. Remove from heat. In a bowl, mix flour, remaining sugar, baking powder, salt and milk; stir until smooth. Add flour mixture to butter in baking pan; carefully add berry mixture. Bake at 400 degrees for 25 to 30 minutes, until bubbly and crust is golden.

★ PENNY PINCHER ★ For an affordable casual get-together, invite friends over for "just desserts!" Offer two or three simple homebaked desserts like cobblers, dump cake and fruit pie, ice cream for topping and a steamy pot of coffee...they'll love it!.

Wild Blackberry Cobbler

Kathy White, Cato, NY

Nathaniel's Chocolate Bowl

Any day is a special occasion to fix what your family loves!

Serves 10 to 12

15-1/4 oz. pkg. devil's food cake mix
1 c. water
1/2 c. oil
3 eggs, beaten
2 3.4-oz. pkgs. instant chocolate
  pudding mix
4 c. milk
16-oz. container frozen whipped
  topping, thawed
1 c. mini semi-sweet chocolate chips

Prepare cake mix with water, oil and eggs according to package directions; bake in a greased 13"x9" baking pan. Cool completely; cut into one-inch cubes. Meanwhile, prepare pudding mixes with milk according to package directions. In a large glass trifle bowl, layer half each of cake cubes, pudding and whipped topping. Repeat layers, ending with topping. Sprinkle with chocolate chips. Cover and chill until serving time.

★ TIME-SAVING SHORTCUT ★
Just for fun, layer fresh berries with creamy chocolate pudding in stemmed glasses for a festive dessert quick as a wink.

Nathaniel's Chocolate Bowl

Carole Akers, Bellevue, OH

Butter Pecan Peach Cake

So refreshing in the summer, or serve warm on chilly days...a yummy treat either way!

Serves 18 to 24

29-oz. can sliced peaches
18-1/4 oz. pkg. butter pecan or yellow
  cake mix
1/2 c. butter, melted
1 c. chopped pecans
1 c. sweetened flaked coconut

Pour peaches and syrup in the bottom of an ungreased 13"x9" baking pan. Cover with dry cake mix; drizzle butter over the top. Sprinkle with pecans and coconut. Bake, uncovered, at 350 degrees for 30 to 35 minutes.

Denise Crowser, Canby, MN

Homemade Chocolate Pudding

My mother made this pudding for our family at least once a week when we were growing up. It's heavenly with a scoop of vanilla ice cream melting in the hot pudding!

Makes 6 servings

2/3 c. sugar
1/3 c. cornstarch
3 T. baking cocoa
3 c. milk
2 T. margarine, softened
1 t. vanilla extract

Sift together dry ingredients in a medium saucepan. Add cold milk; mix well. Bring to a boil over medium heat; cook until thickened, stirring constantly. Remove from heat. Add margarine and vanilla; mix well. Serve warm.

Butter Pecan Peach Cake

Debbie Desormeaux, Lafayette, LA

First-Prize Peach Cobbler

Our family loves this! It tastes great served warm or cold.

Serves 6 to 8

18-1/2 oz. pkg. yellow cake mix
29-oz. can sliced peaches
15-oz. can sliced peaches
1/2 c. half-and-half
1/2 c. sugar
1/2 c. butter, sliced
Garnish: whipped cream or
   vanilla ice cream

Add dry cake mix to a 13"x9" baking pan sprayed with non-stick vegetable spray. Make a well in the center of cake mix. Add undrained peaches and half-and-half; stir to blend and moisten. Sprinkle with sugar; dot with butter. Cover and refrigerate 8 hours to overnight to allow flavors to blend. Bake at 350 degrees for one hour, or until bubbly and golden. Serve warm or cold, garnished as desired.

Christy Bonner, Berry, AL

Chocolate Cobbler

This is a treasured family recipe that has been passed down for many years...a rich, scrumptious treat for chocolate lovers!

Serves 12 to 14

3/4 c. margarine, melted
1-1/2 c. self-rising flour
2-1/2 c. sugar, divided
1/2 c. plus 1 T. baking cocoa, divided
3/4 c. milk
1 t. vanilla extract
2-1/4 c. boiling water

Spread margarine in a 13"x9" glass baking pan; set aside. Combine flour, one cup sugar, 3 tablespoons cocoa, milk and vanilla; pour into pan. Mix together remaining sugar and cocoa; sprinkle over top. Pour boiling water over top; do not stir. Bake at 350 degrees for 40 to 45 minutes. Makes 12 to 14 servings.

★ STORE IT ★ Stock up on cake mixes, pudding mixes and fruit pie fillings whenever they go on sale...mix & match to make all kinds of simply delicious desserts.

First-Prize Peach Cobbler

Niki Baltz, Zionsville, IN

Pecan Balls with Fudge Sauce

My mother-in-law taught me to make this scrumptious dessert when I was a newlywed.

Serves 8 to 10

1/2 gal. vanilla ice cream, softened
2 c. chopped pecans
Optional: frozen whipped topping, thawed, and maraschino cherries

Scoop ice cream into 8 to 10 orange-size balls. Roll in pecans; place in a baking pan, cover and freeze. At serving time, top with Fudge Sauce and, if desired, whipped topping and cherries.

Fudge Sauce:

1/2 c. butter
2 1-oz. sqs. unsweetened baking chocolate
2/3 c. sugar
1/2 c. evaporated milk
1/2 t. vanilla extract

Melt butter and chocolate in a saucepan over low heat. Add sugar; stir about 2 to 3 minutes, until smooth. Immediately add evaporated milk and vanilla; mix well and bring to a slow boil. Remove from heat; let cool before pouring over Pecan Balls.

★ SAVVY SECRET ★ Invite friends & family to an old-fashioned ice cream social! Serve Pecan Balls with lots of toppings...fluffy whipped cream, peanuts, bananas, maraschino cherries, hot fudge sauce and butterscotch topping. Give a prize for the most creative sundae!

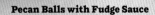

Pecan Balls with Fudge Sauce

Andrea Ford, Montfort, WI

Marshmallow Graham Custard

I first made this recipe when I was a little girl. I loved it then and still make it to this day.

Makes 4 servings

1-1/2 c. milk
1/3 c. graham cracker crumbs, finely ground
2 eggs, beaten
2 T. sugar
1/8 t. salt
1/2 t. vanilla extract
8 marshmallows, quartered

In a large bowl, pour milk over cracker crumbs; set aside. In a separate bowl, combine eggs, sugar, salt and vanilla; stir into milk mixture. Stir in marshmallows and pour into 4 ungreased custard cups. Set cups in a shallow pan of hot water. Bake at 325 degrees for 40 minutes, or until a knife inserted in the center comes out clean.

Stephanie Mayer, Portsmouth, VA

Baked Custard

Creamy and comforting...top with a dollop of whipped cream and a dash of nutmeg.

Makes 4 servings

1 c. evaporated milk
1 c. water
4 egg yolks
1/3 c. sugar
1/4 t. salt
1/2 t. vanilla extract

Combine milk and water in a saucepan; heat just to boiling and set aside. Beat yolks slightly; add sugar, salt and vanilla. Gradually add hot milk to eggs, stirring constantly. Divide into 4 custard cups; set in a pan of hot water. Bake at 325 degrees for 50 minutes, or until a knife tip comes out clean. Serve warm or chilled.

★ DOUBLE DUTY ★ Pull out those fanciful, flowery teacups tucked away for "someday." They're just the right size for holding sweet servings of custards, bread puddings and cobblers.

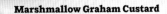
Marshmallow Graham Custard

Sharon Demers, Dolores, CO

Cherry-Pecan Bread Pudding

My husband loves bread pudding! I've tried recipe after recipe until I came up with this one...we think it's perfect!

Serves 8 to 10

2-lb. loaf French bread or homestyle white bread, cubed
4 c. milk
2 c. half-and-half
3/4 c. plus 2 T. sugar, divided
6 eggs, beaten
2 t. vanilla extract
1/2 t. cinnamon
1/2 c. dried tart cherries
1/2 c. chopped pecans
1/2 c. butter, melted

Spread bread cubes on a baking sheet; let dry overnight. In a saucepan over low heat, combine milk, half-and-half and 7 tablespoons sugar. Heat to 120 degrees on a candy thermometer; remove from heat. In a large bowl, combine eggs, vanilla, cinnamon and remaining sugar; blend with a whisk. Stir in cherries and pecans. Slowly whisk half of milk mixture into egg mixture; add remaining milk mixture. Stir in bread cubes; toss to mix and let stand for 5 minutes. Mix in melted butter; transfer mixture to a lightly greased 13"x10" baking pan. Bake at 350 degrees for 35 minutes, or until center is firm. Serve warm.

★ FREEZE IT ★ **Tuck odds & ends of leftover cinnamon rolls, fruit muffins and doughnuts into a freezer container...they're scrumptious in your favorite bread pudding recipe.**

Cherry-Pecan Bread Pudding

DESSERTS IN A BOWL

Becky Holsinger, Belpre, OH

Pineapple-Cherry Crisp

Quick & easy to make, and most of the ingredients can be kept in the pantry for a spur-of-the-moment treat. Can't beat that!

Serves 12 to 15

20-oz. can crushed pineapple, well drained
2 21-oz. cans cherry pie filling
18-1/2 oz. pkg. white cake mix
1/2 c. butter, thinly sliced
3/4 c. chopped pecans
Garnish: whipped cream or ice cream

Spread pineapple evenly in an ungreased 13"x9" baking pan. Spoon pie filling over pineapple. Sprinkle dry cake mix on top; dot with butter and top with pecans. Bake at 350 degrees for 45 minutes, or until bubbly and topping is golden. Serve warm or cooled, garnished as desired.

Margie Fischer, Sun Valley, CA

Down-Home Apple Dumplings

A real old-fashioned treat! This is a dessert dumpling, but we've always enjoyed these served with our meal as a side dish.

Makes 4 servings

1 c. sugar
1 c. water
1/8 t. cinnamon
1/8 t. nutmeg
2 T. butter
2 c. all-purpose flour
2 t. baking powder
1 t. salt
2/3 c. shortening
1/2 c. milk
3 apples, peeled, cored and sliced
Garnish: sugar, cinnamon, nutmeg, diced butter

Combine sugar, water and spices in a saucepan; bring to a boil. Add butter and set aside. Mix together flour, baking powder and salt in a medium bowl; cut in shortening. Add milk; stir until moistened. Roll out 1/4-inch thick on a lightly floured surface; cut into 4-inch squares. Divide apple slices among squares; sprinkle with sugar and spices and dot with butter. Bring all 4 corners together in center; pinch together. Arrange dumplings in a greased 13"x9" baking pan; pour sugar syrup over top. Sprinkle with additional sugar. Bake at 375 degrees for 35 minutes.

Pineapple-Cherry Crisp

Sara Plott, Monument, CO

Hot Fudge Spoon Cake

Heavenly!

Makes 6 servings

1 c. all-purpose flour
1-3/4 c. brown sugar, packed and
   divided
1/4 c. plus 3 T. baking cocoa, divided
2 t. baking powder
1/4 t. salt
1/2 c. milk
2 T. butter, melted
1/2 t. vanilla extract
1-3/4 c. hot water
Optional: vanilla ice cream

Combine flour, one cup brown sugar, 3 tablespoons cocoa, baking powder and salt in a medium bowl. Whisk in milk, butter and vanilla. Spread evenly in a slow cooker. Mix together remaining 3/4 cup brown sugar and 1/4 cup cocoa; sprinkle evenly over top of batter. Pour in hot water; do not stir. Cover and cook on high setting for 2 hours or until a toothpick inserted one inch deep comes out clean. Spoon warm cake into bowls; top with vanilla ice cream, if desired.

★ SAVVY SECRET ★ **Fresh whipped cream makes any dessert even more delectable. It's easy too. Combine one cup whipping cream with 1/4 cup powdered sugar and one teaspoon vanilla extract in a chilled bowl. Beat with chilled beaters until stiff peaks form.**

Hot Fudge Spoon Cake

Jodi Wieland, Templeton, IA

Cookies & Cream Dessert

Cookies, pudding and whipped topping...no one can resist this!

Makes 15 servings

14.5-oz. pkg. chocolate sandwich
   cookies, crushed
1/2 c. butter, melted
2 3.4-oz. pkgs. instant vanilla
   pudding mix
3 c. milk
8-oz. pkg. cream cheese, softened
8-oz. container frozen whipped
   topping, thawed
Optional: 8 chocolate sandwich
   cookies, halved

Mix cookie crumbs with butter in a medium bowl; reserve one cup of mixture. Press remaining mixture in the bottom of an ungreased 13"x9" baking pan or individual serving dishes; set aside. In a large bowl, combine pudding mix, milk, cream cheese and whipped topping; spread over cookie crumb mixture. Sprinkle with reserved cookie crumb mixture; refrigerate one hour. Garnish with cookie halves, if desired.

Anna McMaster, Portland, OR

Brownie Pudding Trifle

I use my prettiest cut-glass bowl for this luscious layered dessert.

Makes 12 servings

20-oz. pkg. brownie mix
3.9-oz. pkg. instant chocolate
   pudding mix
14-oz. can sweetened condensed
   milk
1/2 c. water
16-oz. container frozen whipped
   topping, thawed and divided

Bake brownie mix according to package instructions. Cool completely; cut into one-inch squares and set aside. In a large bowl, combine pudding mix, condensed milk and water; stir until smooth. Fold in 3 cups whipped topping. In a glass serving bowl, layer half the brownies, half the pudding mixture and half the remaining whipped topping. Repeat layering. Chill for 8 hours or overnight before serving.

Cookies & Cream Dessert

Marcia Marcoux, Charlton, MA

Creamy Raspberry Mousse

It's a snap to make this elegant dessert.

Makes 6 servings

1-1/2 c. white chocolate chips
1 c. milk
12-oz. pkg. frozen raspberries, thawed
2 to 3 T. sugar
2 3.9-oz. pkgs. white chocolate instant pudding mix
2 c. frozen whipped topping, thawed
Optional: 1/2 c. chopped pistachios

Combine white chocolate chips and milk in a large microwave-safe bowl. Microwave on high 15 seconds at a time, stirring between each interval, until chips are melted. Place in refrigerator until cold; stir occasionally to minimize separation. Process raspberries and sugar in a blender until smooth. Strain seeds, if desired; set aside. When chocolate mixture is cold, add pudding mix; beat with an electric mixer at medium speed about 2 minutes. Fold in whipped topping; refrigerate at least one hour. Divide among 6 individual serving bowls; top each with about 2 tablespoons of raspberry mixture. Sprinkle with pistachios, if desired.

★ SIMPLE INGREDIENT SWAP ★ **Prefer blueberries over raspberries? Try this simple sauce instead. Combine 2 c. frozen blueberries, 1/3 c. water, 1/4 c. sugar, and 2 T. lemon juice in a small pan over medium-high heat. Bring to a boil, then lower heat and simmer. Combine 1-1/2 T. cornstarch with 2 T. water until dissolved. Stir into blueberries. Simmer until sauce thickens. Cool before serving.**

Creamy Raspberry Mousse

Jeannie Wolf, Findlay, OH

Virginia Apple Pudding

My mom would make this in the fall when apples were plentiful. It was especially good on a chilly evening... I remember eating leftovers for breakfast too!

Serves 4 to 6

2-1/4 c. apples, peeled, cored and sliced
1/2 c. butter, sliced
1 c. sugar
1 c. all-purpose flour
2 t. baking powder
1/4 t. salt
1/4 t. cinnamon
1 c. milk
Garnish: whipped cream, ice cream or lemon sauce

In a saucepan, cover apples with water. Cook over medium-high heat just until tender, about 5 minutes; drain well. Place butter in a 2-quart casserole dish; melt in oven at 375 degrees. In a bowl, stir together remaining ingredients except garnish; pour over butter in dish. Do not stir. Spoon apples into center of batter; do not stir. Bake at 375 degrees for about 40 minutes, until batter covers fruit and crust forms. Serve warm or cold; garnish as desired.

Liz Gatewood, Madison, IN

Creamy Banana Pudding

My dear friend Barb gave me this recipe many years ago...I think of her every time I make it.

Serves 8 to 10

5-1/4 oz. pkg. instant vanilla pudding mix
2 c. milk
14-oz. can sweetened condensed milk
12-oz. container frozen whipped topping, thawed
12-oz. pkg. vanilla wafers
4 to 5 bananas, sliced

Combine pudding mix, milks and topping in a large bowl; mix together until well blended. Spoon one cup of pudding mixture into a large glass serving bowl. Layer with one-third each of wafers, banana slices and remaining pudding mixture. Repeat layers twice, ending with pudding mixture. Chill; keep refrigerated.

Virginia Apple Pudding

Index

Mains-Vegetarian

Salads

Smoothies

Soups

U. S. to Metric Recipe Equivalents

Volume Measurements

¼ teaspoon	....	1 mL
½ teaspoon	....	2 mL
1 teaspoon	....	5 mL
1 tablespoon = 3 teaspoons	....	15 mL
2 tablespoons = 1 fluid ounce	....	30 mL
¼ cup	....	60 mL
⅓ cup	....	75 mL
½ cup = 4 fluid ounces	....	125 mL
1 cup = 8 fluid ounces	....	250 mL
2 cups = 1 pint = 16 fluid ounces	..	500 mL
4 cups = 1 quart	....	1 L

Weights

1 ounce	....	30 g
4 ounces	....	120 g
8 ounces	....	225 g
16 ounces = 1 pound	....	450 g

Baking Pan Sizes

Square

8x8x2 inches	....	2 L = 20x20x5 cm
9x9x2 inches	....	2.5 L = 23x23x5 cm

Rectangular

13x9x2 inches	....	3.5 L = 33x23x5 cm

Loaf

9x5x3 inches	....	2 L = 23x13x7 cm

Round

8x1-1/2 inches	....	1.2 L = 20x4 cm
9x1-1/2 inches	....	1.5 L = 23x4 cm

Recipe Abbreviations

t. = teaspoon	ltr. = liter
T. = tablespoon	oz. = ounce
c. = cup	lb. = pound
pt. = pint	doz. = dozen
qt. = quart	pkg. = package
gal. = gallon	env. = envelope

Oven Temperatures

300° F	....	150° C
325° F	....	160° C
350° F	....	180° C
375° F	....	190° C
400° F	....	200° C
450° F	....	230° C

Kitchen Measurements

A pinch = ⅛ tablespoon
1 fluid ounce = 2 tablespoons
3 teaspoons = 1 tablespoon
4 fluid ounces = ½ cup
2 tablespoons = ⅛ cup
8 fluid ounces = 1 cup
4 tablespoons = ¼ cup
16 fluid ounces = 1 pint
8 tablespoons = ½ cup
32 fluid ounces = 1 quart
16 tablespoons = 1 cup
16 ounces net weight = 1 pound
2 cups = 1 pint
4 cups = 1 quart
4 quarts = 1 gallon